FRENCH GRAMMAR

This comprehensive introduction to the principles of French grammar is intended for the student who has a basic grounding in French but who wishes to gain a further understanding of its grammatical structure. Each component of the sentence is lucidly explained and practical examples are included in each case. The comprehensive contents list also makes this an ideal revision and reference text.

TEACH YOURSELF BOOKS

FRENCH GRAMMAR

E. S. Jenkins, B.A.

TEACH YOURSELF BOOKS
Hodder and Stoughton

First printed 1961
Nineteenth impression 1984

Copyright © 1961
Hodder and Stoughton Ltd

ISBN 0 340 26170 6

Printed in Great Britain
for Hodder and Stoughton Educational, a division of
Hodder and Stoughton Ltd, Mill Road, Dunton Green,
Sevenoaks, Kent
by Richard Clay (The Chaucer Press) Ltd, Bungay, Suffolk

CONTENTS

ACKNOWLEDGMENT

The author would like to express his gratitude to his colleagues V. A. Cullingworth, Esq., M.A., W. N. Jeeves, Esq., M.A., and Monsieur A. Theil, L. ès L. for their help and suggestions and also to the Editor-in-Chief, Leonard Cutts, Esq., for his kindness and encouragement.

PREFACE

This Grammar is not intended for absolute beginners who are learning a language for the first time. The reader should have worked conscientiously through a course such as *Teach Yourself French* or already made some progress in the language.

It has been written with certain purposes in mind. It is fairly exhaustive, but the author hopes that one will not find it exhausting. Much has been included that could have been left out: it is possible to make oneself understood with a bare minimum of grammatical knowledge. However, this is an inquiring age, and a student may well wish to find out the reason for certain turns of phrase in the works of some of the great authors. It therefore follows that the learner must not be disheartened if he cannot at once remember all the points in a book like this. If he did, he would know more about French grammar than the average Frenchman. In practice, he will discover that the grammatical puzzles which give him difficulty are the very ones that also trouble the native speaker.

It is hoped that the book will be used in two ways. First, that it will be read as a book from cover to cover or at least from beginning to end of a chapter: secondly, that it will serve as a reference. It will then explain a baffling sentence and help the student to speak and write French correctly. With these aims in view, we have set out at the beginning of the book a comprehensive list of contents. However, we must warn you that a grammar cannot include everything, and a good dictionary should never be far away.

French is a difficult language to write elegantly and correctly, and any attempt to gloss over this fact would be unfair to the student. However, even French people have sometimes to content themselves with something short of perfection, so we hope that this will help to console anyone worried about making a mistake. Your French *vis-à-vis* may be quite as uncertain about the correct preposition or tense as you are yourself!

To write a grammar book without using grammatical terms is an impossibility. Every branch of knowledge has its jargon, and the reader will learn more quickly if he knows the difference between a noun, a verb and an adjective. In fact, grammatical terms have been kept to a minimum, and if any explanation proves difficult there is always an example together with a translation to help.

The author has made an honest attempt to include the fruits of many years of teaching the French language. He hopes that this volume will prove of some benefit to all students.

INTRODUCTION

THE ORIGINS OF THE FRENCH LANGUAGE

Most French words are of Latin origin. During the first centuries of the Christian era, Roman soldiers, colonists and traders introduced into Gaul a popular kind of Latin which was very different from that used by Virgil, Cicero and Caesar. This gradually supplanted the native languages and slowly changed into a tongue called Gallo-Roman. Later, in the Middle Ages, many words were introduced by scholars who borrowed them from Classical Latin. In this way the same Latin word might be taken into French twice: for instance, auscultare became écouter in early popular speech and ausculter in later learned form. Naturally enough, the involved grammar of classical Latin was much simplified when it was brought into Gaul: Latin cases were dropped, declensions were reduced in number, tenses were more simply formed. This tendency increased with the passing of the years.

By the ninth century the various dialects spoken throughout the country had become two great groups: in the north that of the langue d'oïl, in the south the langue d'oc (so called because oïl and oc were their respective ways of saying 'yes'). Very gradually, between the twelfth and sixteenth centuries, the dialect spoken round Paris, in the region called the Ile de France, became the most important, mainly because it was there that the royal family lived.

As for the native language of Gaul, it had disappeared more or less completely by the end of the fourth century. Only a few traces remain in modern French—a handful of words and the method of counting in twenties.*

* This Celtic system of numbering has survived in France for the numbers 61 to 99. In the French-speaking parts of Switzerland septante (70), huitante (80) and nonante (90) are used: in Belgium septante (70) and nonante (90).

Like other European languages, French has also borrowed from Classical Greek, from the Frankish invaders in the fifth century and extensively in modern times from English and American. It is not surprising either, when we consider France's geographical position and political evolution, to find Scandinavian, Dutch, Italian, Spanish and Arabic words well represented in French.

Spelling

French is fairly logical in its spelling and not nearly so capricious as English. However, from the learner's point of view, it is quite bad enough. A word is not always pronounced as it is spelt, there are accents to deal with, and parasitical consonants like *h* which are never sounded. Two other examples of the latter tendency are the *p* in sculpteur (pronounced *sculteur*) and the *g* and *t* in doigt (pronounced *doi*).

Use of the Hyphen

The hyphen is used:

1. In certain compound words: demi-heure, half-hour; avant-coureur, forerunner.

2. Between the verb and the personal pronoun in the Interrogative and Imperative Affirmative: parle-t-il? is he speaking?; dites-le-moi! say it to me!

3. Between the emphatic pronoun and the adjective même: lui-même, himself.

4. In compound numbers from 17 to 99 inclusive: quatre-vingts, eighty; vingt-six, twenty-six.

5. With the particles -ci, -là in cases like celui-ci, this one; cet homme-là, that man.

6. With certain expressions: pêle-mêle, higgledy-piggledy; au-delà, beyond.

Use of Capital Letters

The capital letter is more rarely used in French than in English. It is found:

1. With the first word of a sentence or direct speech:

Il a demandé: "Où avez-vous trouvé ce livre?" He asked: "Where did you find this book?"

2. With proper names: Jean Dupont, la France, la Seine.

3. With words like Dieu, God; Jésus, Jesus; le Seigneur, the Lord; la Vierge, the Blessed Virgin, etc.

4. With names of societies, organisations, etc.: L'Église, the Church; la Chambre des Députés, the House of Commons, le Ministère de la Justice, the Ministry of Justice.

5. With the names of feasts: Noël, Christmas; Pâques, Easter.

6. With titles of nobility or distinction: Sa Majesté, His Majesty; Monsieur le Président, Mr. President.

7. For titles of books, plays, pictures etc.: la Joconde, the Mona Lisa; Antigone, Antigone.

The capital letter is not used:

1. For adjectives of nationality: une ville française, a French town.

2. For names of languages: il apprend l'allemand, he is learning German.

3. For words like rue, street; place, square, etc.: il demeure rue Lepic, he lives in Lepic Street.

4. In monsieur, madame, mademoiselle, etc., with a name unless the words are abbreviated: avec un monsieur, but avec M. Boussion.

The Apostrophe

The vowels *a, e* are replaced by an apostrophe when le, la, je, me, te, se, ce que, de, ne come before a vowel or mute *h*: l'an, the year; j'ai, I have; je m'excuse, I excuse myself; il t'ennuie, he annoys you.

Similarly, lorsque, puisque, quoique lose their final *e* when followed by il, ils, elle, elles, un, une, on: puisqu'il est là, since he is there.

Jusque loses its *e* in jusqu'à, up to, until; jusqu'alors, up till then; jusqu'ici, up to now; jusqu'où, up to where; jusqu'au bout, to the end.

Quelque keeps its *e* except in the word quelqu'un, some-one.

Presque keeps its *e* except in presqu'île, peninsula.

Si, if, drops the *i* before il, ils: s'il arrive, if he arrives, but keeps it before elle, elles, on: si elle chante, if she sings.

In the Imperative Affirmative and the Interrogative, when je, le, la, ce come after the verb, there is no elision: puis-je entrer? may I come in?; est-ce ici? is it here?; donnez-le à votre soeur! give it to your sister!

Note the absence of the *e* in words like grand'rue, high-street; grand'mère, grandmother.

Diaeresis

This sign is used to show that contiguous vowels are to be pronounced separately and not to be combined into a diphthong. Thus naïf, (*na-ïf*), naive; Moïse, (*Mo-ïse*), Moses. In words like aiguë the sign shows that the word has two syllables ai-guë (pronounced *ay-gee*), acute.

Cedilla

The cedilla is used when it is necessary to give *c* the sound of *s* before the vowels *a*, *o*, *u*:

un Français, a Frenchman; nous commençons, we begin; conçu, conceived.

Punctuation

A comma is used in French for the English decimal point: 3,06 stands for our 3·06 (three point nought six). In figures the French put a full stop where we have a comma: 4.606 represents our 4,606 (four thousand six hundred and six).

Inverted commas to mark speech or to emphasise words are shown thus «   »:

«Donnez-le-moi!» dit-il. "Give it to me!", he said.

Accents

Accents are small signs written over vowels. They are used in two ways:

1. To indicate the pronunciation—

(*a*) An acute accent is put over the letter *e* to show it is pronounced something like the English *ay*; the phonetic symbol for this sound is e. Thus l'été, the summer; la gelée, frost.

(*b*) A grave accent placed over the letter *e* shows that è is to be pronounced like *e* in the English word "bet": the phonetic symbol is ɛ: la mère, the mother; il lève, he lifts.

(*c*) The circumflex accent generally lengthens the vowel: le mât, the mast; même, even, same.

2. Accents can also serve as a useful distinction between words otherwise indistinguishable in spelling and pronunciation: la, the; là, there; du, of the; dû, owed; ou, or; où, where.

h at the Beginning of a Word

The letter *h* should never be sounded in French. Most words beginning with *h* are treated as if the *h* did not exist at all and therefore elide the vowels *a* and *e* in the article: l'horizon, the horizon; l'humidité, wetness, etc. Some words begin with a so-called "aspirate" *h*, though in fact it is not sounded at all. All that happens is that the *h* is treated as if it were a proper consonant, with the result that there is no elision and no liaison before it. Thus la haie, the hedge; le haricot, the bean, with their plurals les haies, les haricots, where the *s* in les is not pronounced. In fact, a slight pause may be made between the preceding word and the word beginning with the aspirate *h*. This particular type of *h*, which occurs only at the beginning of a French word, is usually marked in a dictionary by a special sign, frequently an asterisk. To make a mistake over an aspirate *h* sounds just as bad to a Frenchman as a dropped aitch sounds to an Englishman.

The French Alphabet

French uses the same alphabet as we do, but the letter *w* is used only in words borrowed from other languages: **le wagon-lit**, sleeping-car; **le week-end**, the week-end; **le sandwich**, the sandwich; **le whist**, whist.

Division of a French Word into Syllables

The main distinction between English pronunciation and French is that we end a syllable with a consonant, whereas the French begin with a consonant. Thus, in very slow speech, we should say PAP-A, a Frenchman would say PA-PA. Compare **mo-dèle**, **pré-fé-rer**, **l'A-mé-rique** with the English mod-el, pref-er, Am-er-ic-a. When there are two consonants they are generally separated: **par-ler**, to speak; **quel-que**, some; **por-ta-tif**, portable, but if the second of the two consonants is *l* or *r* both consonants begin the syllable (except *rl, nr, nl*): **pro-gramme**, program; **tien-dra**, will hold.

Liaison

A feature of French pronunciation is the habit of running several words together. **Y en a-t-il?**, for instance, is sounded as if it were one single word. This joining of words is called in French liaison. It is useful to note that in liaison the letter *d* is pronounced as a *t*: **un grand homme**; *s* and *x* sound like *z*: **les hommes, deux enfants.**

When to make liaison

1. Between articles and nouns: **les enfants, les hommes, un exercice, des années.**

2. Between adjectives and following nouns: **un grand homme, mes enfants, le nouvel an.**

3. Between pronouns and verbs: **il y en a, cherchent-ils?, ils ont parlé.**

4. Between auxiliary and verb and after **avoir** and **être: vous avez été, ils sont arrivés, vous avez une plume, nous sommes innocents.**

5. After many prepositions, conjunctions and adverbs in a sense group of words: **en un instant, quand elle viendra, bien heureux, très aimable.**

6. Plural nouns generally pronounce the *s* or *x* before a following vowel: **des chevaux énormes.**

7. Between numerals and nouns: **trois années, vingt hommes.**

Do not try to make too many liaisons. It is better to make too few than too many.

When to avoid liaison

1. Do not make a liaison after a singular noun: do not, for instance, pronounce the *t* in a phrase like **un goût amer.**

2. The *t* in et is never sounded: **un homme et une femme.**

3. Do not make a liaison before **oui, onze, huit: mais oui, les onze joueurs, mes huit valises.**

CHAPTER I
THE NOUN

A noun is the name of a person, place or thing. The words Peter, England, book, silver, charity, pneumonia, rugby are all nouns.

Masculine and Feminine Gender

French nouns are divided into two genders—masculine and feminine. There is no neuter; to a Frenchman everything is a "he" or a "she". As a general rule, male animate beings are masculine, **le taureau**, the bull, while female animate beings are feminine, **la vache**, the cow. Very often, however, and especially in the case of smaller animals, no such distinction is made: i.e., **le ver**, the worm (masculine); **la panthère**, the panther (feminine). With inanimate things and abstractions there is no logical reason for the gender except form, analogy and etymology.

Before we go further let us remember that many other languages are similarly burdened with gender. For those who have learned Latin, it is useful to remember that masculine or feminine nouns usually kept their gender on becoming French. Neuter nouns generally became masculine. Mistakes in gender are serious, so you should endeavour to learn the gender of each noun as you come across it. Here are some rules which may prove helpful:

Gender Depending on the Meaning of the Word

(a) *Masculines*

1. Names of metals, trees, months, days of the week, seasons, languages: **le fer**, iron; **le chêne**, the oak; **le décembre**, December; **le dimanche**, Sunday; **le printemps**, Spring; **le français**, French.

2. Adjectives and Infinitives used as nouns: l'intérieur, the inside; le sourire, the smile.

3. Names of countries and towns not ending in *e*: le Portugal, Portugal; le Danemark, Denmark; le Japon, Japan.

(b) *Feminines*

1. Names of countries and towns ending in *e*: la France, France; l'Allemagne, Germany; la Suisse, Switzerland.

2. Flowers, fruits and vegetables ending in *e*: la rose, the rose; la pomme, the apple; la carotte, the carrot.

3. Names of festivals: la Pentecôte, Whitsun; la Toussaint, All Saints' Day. (La fête* is the French for festival.)

4. Names of sciences: la grammaire, grammar; la chimie, Chemistry; la physique, Physics.

Gender of the Letters of the Alphabet

The vowels are masculine, and the tendency is to make all the consonants masculine too, though some writers make them feminine if they sound as if they began with a vowel: thus un b, un c, un d, une f, un g, une h, etc.

Gender of Compound Nouns

In compound nouns such as le chef d'œuvre, masterpiece, the noun is masculine because the main part of it, le chef, is of that gender. Likewise la basse-cour, farmyard, is feminine because cour, yard, is feminine. Similar words are le bateau-mouche, m., passenger boat on the Seine; la chauve-souris, f., bat, whose gender depends on the fact that le bateau is masculine and la souris is feminine. On the other hand, such compounds as le tête-à-tête, confidential conversation (lit. "head to head"), and le passe-partout,

* This explains expressions like la mi-août, mid-August because one thinks of la fête de l'Assomption, Assumption Day, August 15. Following this pattern, we have la mi-février, mid-February; la mi-janvier and la mi-temps, half-time.

master-key (lit. "passes everywhere"), are so mixed up as to make any logical gender impossible. When the word is formed of a verb and a noun or a preposition and a noun it is usually masculine: le porte-plume, penholder (lit. "carries pen"); le sous-main, blotting pad (lit. "under the hand").

Gender Depending on the Ending of the Word

There are also characteristic masculine and feminine endings. Here are some masculine terminations: age, ail, eau, ège, eil, ice, ier, ment, oir, our: le ménage, household; le ruisseau, stream; l'artifice, artifice; le dentier, denture; le bâtiment, building; le trottoir, pavement; le tour, the trick. However, exceptions occur, the most common of which are la page, page (of a book); la cage, cage; la plage, beach; l'image, picture; l'eau, water; la peau, skin; la police, police; la jument, mare; la tour, tower; la cour, court or yard, all of which are feminine.

Similarly, the following are considered to be feminine endings: ade, aille, aison, ance, ée, eille, ence, esse, ette, ie, ière, ille, ion, ise, té, tié, tion, tude, ue, ure. Thus la bataille, battle; la saison, season; la chance, luck; la brassée, armful; la bouteille, bottle; l'insolence, insolence; la pie, magpie; la beauté, beauty; la gratitude, gratitude; la levure, yeast. Exceptions of course exist, among which we should note le lycée, grammar-school; le musée, museum; le silence, silence; le squelette, skeleton; le parapluie, umbrella; l'incendie, fire; le cimetière, cemetery, le murmure, murmur.

Nouns with Masculine and Feminine Forms

Often there is one word for the female of the species and another for the male. Here are a few well-known examples: le bouc, he-goat, la chèvre, nanny-goat; le cheval, horse, l'étalon, stallion, la jument, mare; le coq, cock, la poule, hen; le fils, son, la fille, daughter; le frère, brother, la sœur, sister; le gendre, son-in-law, la bru, daughter-in-law; le héros, hero, l'héroïne, heroine; le mari, husband, la femme, wife; le neveu, nephew, la nièce, niece; le parrain, godfather, la marraine, godmother; le taureau, bull, la vache, cow.

Nouns with One Form for Both Sexes

Others have only one form for both sexes: enfant, child; élève, pupil; artiste, artist; esclave, slave; hypocrite, hypocrite. We may therefore say un enfant (m.) or une enfant (f.); un élève or une élève, a male child, a female child, a boy pupil, a girl pupil, etc. With animals it is usual to add the words mâle or femelle, i.e., la souris mâle, male mouse, la souris femelle, female mouse. In the case of words which were once exclusively applied to men, the emancipation of women has led to difficulties. For some words like académicien, member of an academy; aviateur, airman; avocat, barrister; instituteur, teacher; there are feminine forms like académicienne, aviatrice, avocate, institutrice. For others, like auteur, author; écrivain, writer; professeur, professor or Grammar School master; imposteur, impostor; médecin, doctor of medicine; témoin, witness; sculpteur, sculptor; peintre, painter; there is no feminine. One is forced to say une femme auteur, a woman author; une femme écrivain, docteur, professeur if one wants to make oneself clear. In titles one writes Madame le docteur X or Madame X, docteur en médecine, etc. Otherwise one uses the masculine form: Cette femme est un imposteur mais c'est un grand écrivain. Elle a été mon professeur *: This woman is an impostor but she is a great writer. She was my Professor. However, in speaking of the wife of a prefect or general, one can say Madame la préfète or Madame la générale. Conversely, some words have no masculine forms, so that a man may be une personne, a person; une victime, a victim; une connaissance, an acquaintance; or une dupe, a dupe.

---

* It is interesting to note that in familiar speech, expressions like mon petit, mon chéri can be used when speaking to a woman.

Making a Masculine Word into Corresponding Feminine

Very often we can make a feminine word out of a masculine by adding an *e*. Thus le cousin, male cousin, la cousine, female cousin; le marquis, marquis, la marquise, marchioness; l'Espagnol, Spaniard, l'Espagnole, Spanish woman; l'ami, friend, l'amie, girl-friend; le marié, groom, la mariée, bride. Sometimes too, the final consonant is modified or doubled: le loup, wolf, la louve, she-wolf; le veuf, widower, la veuve, widow; le chat, cat, la chatte, she-cat; le chien, dog, la chienne, bitch; l'espion, spy, l'espionne, female spy; le Parisien, male inhabitant of Paris, la Parisienne, female inhabitant of Paris. This change of consonant does not always occur: l'avocat, barrister, becomes l'avocate; le chameau, camel turns into la chamelle.

Feminine of Words Ending in -EUR

Words ending in -EUR present a special difficulty. Some, comparative in meaning, add an *e* to the masculine; majeur(e), major; mineur(e), minor; meilleur(e), better; supérieur(e), superior. Others, which have the same stem as the present participle of the verb, change -EUR to -EUSE: voleur, thief, voleuse, woman thief; pêcheur, fisherman, pêcheuse, fisherwoman; vendeur, salesman, vendeuse, saleswoman. There are also a few which have a feminine form in -ERESSE: chasseur, hunter, chasseresse, huntress; pécheur, sinner, pécheresse, female sinner. Words ending in -TEUR, generally learned words, form their feminines in -TRICE: the most common are: acteur, actor, actrice, actress; empereur, emperor, impératrice, empress; lecteur, reader, lectrice, woman reader; protecteur, protector, protectrice, protectress. Enchanteur becomes enchanteresse, and here we might mention a few nouns in -e which have a feminine in -esse: nègre, negro, négresse, negress; comte, count, comtesse, countess; duc, duke, duchesse, duchess.

Nouns Masculine or Feminine According to Meaning

Certain words can be masculine or feminine. The doer of the action may be masculine, the action feminine: un aide, a helper, une aide, help; un critique, a critic, une critique, criticism. Sometimes, the difference in gender entails a difference in meaning. In such cases the similarity between the words may be purely accidental, the two words being derived from two different origins. Thus le livre, the book, la livre, the pound; le manche, the handle, la manche, the sleeve; le mousse, the cabin boy, la mousse, the moss; le page, the page-boy, la page, the page of a book; le poêle, the stove, la poêle, the frying pan; le tour, the trick, la tour, the tower; le vase, the vase, la vase, the mud. It is curious too that while la chose, thing, is feminine, quelque chose, something, is considered masculine: we say quelque chose de nouveau, something new.

Doubtful Gender

In the case of a few nouns, there is a certain amount of doubt concerning their gender. L'après-midi, afternoon, can be either masculine or feminine. L'aigle is masculine when referring to the bird, the eagle, but is feminine when it means a standard or military flag, i.e. "the eagles of Napoleon". Couple is masculine when it stands for a married or engaged couple, feminine when it means "two": une couple d'œufs, a couple of eggs.

Gender of GENS

The word gens needs special attention. Usually it is found in the masculine plural with the sense of "people". However, when an adjective comes immediately before it, this adjective becomes feminine, while any that come after remain masculine. Thus: les vieilles gens, old people, les bonnes gens, good people, and les vieilles gens sont peureux, old people are timid. If the preceding adjective is one that ends in a mute *e*, like honnête or jeune, for instance, the adjective and any other that precede stay masculine: tous les honnêtes gens, all honest people, tous ces gens, all these people.

The Gender of Towns and Ships

What is the gender of towns? When in doubt, we can always evade the issue by saying "la ville de Paris" or "la ville de Metz", in which case you automatically make them feminine for the purposes of agreement. Some, like Le Mans, Le Caire (Cairo), Le Havre, are obviously masculine. Others ending with a mute *e* are generally taken as feminine, thus Rome, Séville, Genève: those like Paris, Dijon are masculine. As for boats and ships, the French Academy has laid down that their names should be of the gender of the word used to distinguish the ship: thus la Normandie, named after the French Province, la Normandie. Despite this, many people use the masculine article, le Normandie, because, after all, it is a ship and both "navire", ship, and "bateau", boat, are masculine.

Plural of Nouns

Putting a noun into the plural presents fewer difficulties. Generally, the sign of the plural is the addition of the letter *s* to the noun: garçon, boy, garçons, boys; livre, book, livres, books. Nouns ending in *s*, *x* or *z* remain unchanged in the plural: un nez, a nose, des nez, noses; un fils, a son, des fils, sons; la noix, the nut, les noix, the nuts. Please remember that this plural *s* is not pronounced in French. Confusion between singular garçon and plural garçons is avoided by the use of an article or other accompanying word: le garçon, les garçons. While we are discussing pronunciation, it is worth while noting that with words like œuf, egg; cerf, stag; bœuf, ox, the *f* is pronounced in the singular but not in the plural. Similarly, the *s* in os, bone, is pronounced in the singular only.

Rules for Formation of the Plural

Not all French nouns take an *s* to form the plural.

1. Words ending in -AL change this termination to -AUX:
le cheval, the horse, les chevaux, the horses; le journal, the
newspaper, les journaux, the newspapers. The most common
exceptions here are bal, ball; carnaval, carnival; chacal,
jackal; festival, festival; régal, feast; récital, recital, which
add *s* to become bals, carnavals, chacals, etc.

2. Words ending in -EU, -AU, -EAU add the letter *x*:
l'oiseau, the bird, les oiseaux; le feu, the fire, les feux. The
principal exceptions are le pneu, tyre, les pneus; le bleu,
bruise, les bleus.

3. The words bail, lease; corail, coral; émail, enamel;
soupirail, air-hole; travail, work; vitrail, stained-glass
window, become in the plural baux, coraux, émaux, soupir-
aux, travaux, vitraux.

4. Seven nouns ending in -OU: bijou, jewel; caillou,
pebble; chou, cabbage; genou, knee; hibou, owl; joujou,
plaything; pou, louse, add *x*: bijoux, cailloux, choux, etc.

Words with two plural forms

The word ciel, sky, can become in the plural cieux or ciels.
Cieux means "the heavens" or "paradise", ciels is used only
in phrases like ciels de tableaux, les ciels de Corot, les beaux
ciels d'Italie, and refers to skies in works of art such as oil-
paintings or climatic and picturesque ones. Œil, eye, becomes in the plural yeux, except in the word œils-de-bœuf,
round windows. Aïeul, grandfather, can form as its plural
aïeux, ancestors, or aïeuls (f. aïeules), grandfathers (f.
grandmothers).

Plural of Compound Nouns

When a word is formed out of two or more elements like
rouge-gorge, redbreast, the question of forming the plural
is rather complicated. In some cases, like gendarme, police-

man; **vaurien**, good for nothing, we simply add an *s* and treat them like any other word: **gendarmes**, **vauriens**. To this class belong nouns like **grand'mère**, plural **grand'mères**. On the other hand, **gentilhomme**, **monsieur**, **madame**, **mademoiselle** become **gentilshommes**, **messieurs**, **mesdames**, **mesdemoiselles**.

When the two elements are separated the sense will help in many cases to decide the formation of the plural:

1. The noun consists of a noun and adjective* or of two nouns in apposition. Both elements become plural: **le chou-fleur**, cauliflower, **les choux-fleurs**; **le sourd-muet**, deaf-mute, **les sourds-muets**; **le cerf-volant**, kite (flying-stag), **les cerfs-volants**. However, learned compounds like **Anglo-Saxon**, **Indo-Chinois**, **Gallo-Romain** take the *s* only on the second element: **Anglo-Saxons**, **Indo-Chinois**, etc.

2. The compound consists of two nouns, one depending on the other with or without a preposition, of the following type: **le chef-d'œuvre**, masterpiece; **l'arc-en-ciel**, the rainbow. The first noun only takes the plural: **le chef-d'œuvre**, **les chefs-d'œuvre**; **l'arc-en-ciel**, **les arcs-en-ciel**: so also **le timbre-poste**, postage stamp, **les timbres-poste**.

In these examples, the use and position of the *s* are quite logical. **Chef-d'œuvre** (lit. chief of work), masterpiece, plural **chefs-d'œuvre**: the *s* is put where it would suit if the word were English, i.e., chiefs of work, masterpieces. Similarly, **arc-en-ciel** (arch in the sky), **arcs-en-ciel** (arches in the sky), rainbows; **timbre-poste**, stamp (of the) post, plural **timbres-poste**, stamps (of the) post.

3. The noun has in it a non-variable element or a verb. This part does not change, the other word takes the plural if the sense demands it. **L'avant-poste**, advanced position, **les avant-postes**, just as we should say in English forepost, foreposts: **le bouche-trou**, stop gap, **les bouche-trous**, stop gaps; **le gratte-ciel**, skyscraper, **les gratte-ciel** (no *s* here

* **demi** (half) in front of the noun is invariable: **une demi-heure**, half an hour, **des demi-heures**.

because **gratte-ciel** means literally "scrape sky", and **a** plural "scrapes-sky" or "scrape-skies" would be ridiculous).

4. Words like le **tête-à-tête**, confidential conversation (lit. head to head), les **tête-à-tête**; le **pick-up**, pick-up, les **pick-up**: le **passe-partout**, pass key (lit. passes everywhere), **les passe-partout** remain invariable. In cases like this the difficulty of fixing the position of the *s* is so great that one just gives up and puts nothing at all!

Plural of Words Borrowed from Other Languages

Some, having become completely French, take the normal plural: un **album**, des **albums**, un **bifteck**, steak, **des biftecks**, un **meeting**, des **meetings**. Latin words like **maximum** have plurals in -*a*, though **maximum** itself can take an *s*. Italian words generally form their plurals in -*i*: **dillettante**, **dillettanti**; **libretto**, **libretti**. Nouns taken from English or American have a tendency, especially as so many people know English, to have their English plurals: un **barman**, **des barmen**; un **sportsman**, des **sportsmen**; un **baby**, **des babies**; un **match**, des **matches** (or **matchs**!), un **sandwich**, **des sandwiches** (or **sandwichs**).

Words Which Have no Plural Form

Family names do not change: Les **Dupont** sont ici, **the** Duponts are here, unless the family is a particularly distinguished one, les **Bourbons**, les **Tudors** or unless the name stands for a type; les **Racines** sont rares, people like Racine are rare. Some parts of speech, such as prepositions, adverbs, etc., when used as nouns do not vary: les **pour** et **les contre**, the pros and the cons; les **non** et les **oui**, the ayes and the nos.

Words Found in the Plural only

Some nouns have no singular form: les **archives**, archives; les **catacombes**, catacombs; les **échecs**, chess; les **vivres**, victuals.

Words Found in the Singular only

Others have no plural: la **botanique**, botany; le **midi**, the south; l'**or**, gold; le **bonheur**, luck; le **vrai**, truth; le **nord**, the north. Lastly must be mentioned words which vary in meaning in singular and plural: la **lunette**, spyglass, les **lunettes**, spectacles.

The student may well find this chapter a very full one. Mistakes in plurals can be made even by those whose native language is French. When in doubt, it is of great value to consult a good dictionary. Make sure that it is a modern one, as practice may change with the passing of the years.

CHAPTER II
THE ARTICLES

THE DEFINITE ARTICLE

The Definite Article corresponds to the English word "the". Unlike the English word, it has many forms as the following table will show:

	Before a masculine word	Before a feminine word	Before a singular word beginning with a vowel or mute h	Before all plurals
THE	LE	LA	L'	LES
OF *FROM* }*THE*	DU	DE LA	DE L'	DES
TO *AT* }*THE*	AU	À LA	À L'	AUX
Thus	le garçon *the boy*	la fillette *the girl*	l'homme *the man*	les ans *the years*
	du film *of the film*	de la femme *of the woman*	de l'eau *of the water*	des gens *of the people*
	au jardin *to the garden*	à la sœur *to the sister*	à l'enfant *to the child*	aux amis *to the friends*

Note the contracted forms **DU, DES, AU** and **AUX.** Formerly **en les** (in the) contracted to **ès**, which is still found in expressions like **docteur ès sciences,** doctor of science; **licencié ès lettres,** bachelor of arts.

You will notice that **LE** and **LA** change to **L'** before a word in the singular beginning with a vowel or a mute *h*: **l'or,** the gold; **l'heure,** the hour.

Initial H Aspirate

Some words, though beginning with the letter *h*, behave as though they began with consonants and have **LE** or **LA**

before them. They include the number huit, eight,* and
other words which, in order to distinguish them, are said to
begin with an aspirate *h*. This *h* is, however, just as silent as
the mute *h*, the letter never being pronounced in French.
Some of the most common of these words are: la hache, axe;
la haie, hedge; la haine, hatred; la halte, halt; le hameau,
hamlet; le hamac, hammock; la hanche, hip; le hangar,
shed; le harem, harem; le haricot, bean; la harpe, harp; le
hasard, luck; la hâte, haste; le havre, haven; le huit mars,
the eighth of March.

Use of the Definite Article

The Definite Article is more often used in French than its
counterpart is in English. As in most cases the pronunciation of the singular noun is the same as that of the plural, the
use of the article is essential to clarify the expression.
Maison, house, maisons, houses, would sound the same in
French, so we must say la maison, les maisons to distinguish
between them. Just compare the following sentences with
their English equivalents:

Horses are useful. Les chevaux sont utiles.
Gold is a metal. L'or est un métal.
Most people. La plupart des gens.

In English, when two or more nouns are used together,
even if the Article is put before the first, it is customary to
leave out the Article before subsequent words. For instance,
we say "the father and mother of this child", "the horses,
cows and sheep are in the field". This must not happen in
French. The Article must be inserted before each noun: le
père et la mère de cet enfant; les chevaux, les vaches et les
moutons sont dans le champ.

The Definite Article is used before the names of countries,
continents, counties and many geographical names: le

* onze, eleven, is similarly used. We say "le onze février", the
eleventh of February.

Portugal, la France, l'Europe, l'Asie, la Normandie, le Kent, le Mont Blanc, le Havre, le Caire (Cairo). However, in the case of feminine nouns of this type, the article is omitted after EN, *to* or *in*, and DE, *from, of*: il va en France, il revient d'Espagne, he is going to France, he comes back from Spain. With masculine nouns of places, the article is retained: Je vais au Havre, au Japon, au Portugal, au Canada, aux Etats-Unis, je reviens du Pays de Galles: I am going to le Havre, Japan, Portugal, Canada, the United States, I come back from Wales.

We use the article:

(*a*) Before abstract nouns, l'argent ne fait pas le bonheur, money does not make happiness.

(*b*) When we have a title and a name, la reine Élisabeth, queen Elizabeth; le président de Gaulle, president de Gaulle, and even when a name is preceded by an adjective: la petite Marie, little Mary; la douce France, sweet land of France.

(*c*) In familiar language the article can be used in front of a name to express scorn: la Dubarry, that woman Dubarry; la Louise, old Louise. On the other hand, used in front of the names of famous woman artistes, it can express respect: la Garbo, la Malibran, la Callas, la Lollobrigida, though this usage seems to be dying out.

(*d*) Notice too the common use of expressions like Monsieur le directeur, Headmaster; messieurs les voyageurs, passengers; monsieur le curé, Vicar, used in addressing people.

(*e*) Feast-days, with the exception of Pâques, Easter, and Noël, Christmas, usually have la before them: Il reviendra à la Trinité, à la Toussaint, à Pâques, à Noël, he will come back on Trinity Sunday, All Saints' Day, Easter, Christmas.

(*f*) When price is mentioned, the French "the" takes the place of the English "a": deux cents francs le kilo, two hundred francs *a* kilo; cent francs la bouteille, a hundred francs *a* bottle; **mille francs le mètre,** a thousand francs *a* yard; **quinze francs (la) pièce,** fifteen francs each (apiece).

(*g*) "Le" is used before days of the week when a customary action is referred to: **il vient ici le lundi,** he comes here of a Monday, on Mondays.

(*h*) The article is used with speeds: **L'auto faisait du cent à l'heure:** The car was doing a hundred (kilometres) *an* hour.

(*i*) The article is placed before the names of languages: **il connaît bien l'allemand,** he knows German well; **il apprend l'italien,** he is learning Italian. However, with the verb **parler,** it is usual to omit it: **ici on parle français,** here one speaks French; **parlez-vous français?,** do you speak French? If, however, you have any additional idea, the article returns: **il parle bien le français,** he speaks French *well*. **Presque tous les Gallois parlent l'anglais:** Nearly all Welsh people speak English (i.e., as well as or instead of their own language).

A very interesting use of the article is to use **au, à la, à l'** or **aux** in translating such expressions as "the man with the wooden leg", "the girl with the big mouth", "the woman with the fair hair". The usual word for "with", **avec,** is not employed because **avec** has the sense of "together with" or "accompanied by", and if put in the examples above would convey the idea of a man carrying a wooden leg, or of a woman with a supply of fair hair which she is about to make into a wig. So, to describe these persons with their characteristics, we say: **l'homme à la jambe de bois, la jeune fille à la grande bouche, la femme aux cheveux blonds.***

The Definite Article is also used in French where in English we should use the possessive adjective, especially with names of parts of the body. Study these examples:

He closes *his* eyes. **Il ferme les yeux.**

She opens *her* mouth. **Elle ouvre la bouche.**

* *a* man with *a* wooden leg = **un homme à jambe de bois.** Similarly *a* woman with fair hair = **une femme à cheveux blonds.**

I rub *my* foot. Je me frotte le pied.
I seized *her* arm. Je lui ai saisi le bras.
They brush *their* hair. Elles se brossent les cheveux.

You will notice that if only one part of the body is involved, if one just moves a limb in a simple, singular movement, we have this type of sentence:

Il ferme les yeux. He closes his eyes.
Elle ouvre la bouche. She opens her mouth.
Il tourne la tête. He turns his head.
Levez la main! Raise your hand!

When an action is done to one part of the body using another, "I scratch my nose (i.e., with my finger)", or if an action is performed on another person, "*I* seized *her* arm", a pronoun must be introduced to show to whom the action is being done.

Il se gratte le nez. He scratches his nose (lit. he scratches to himself the nose).
Je lui ai saisi le bras. I seized her arm (lit. I seized the arm to her).

Unless lui was inserted, we should not know whose arm was seized.

A similar type of sentence is used to describe a person's physical characteristics:

Il a les yeux bleus. He has blue eyes.
Mon frère a le nez long. My brother has a long nose.

Why, then, in view of the above rules, do we sometimes find sentences like the following?

J'admirais ses beaux cheveux. I admired her lovely hair.
Ses mains sont propres. His hands are clean.

The possessive adjectives "her" and "his" must be used here, because otherwise the sentences would mean something quite different. **J'admirais les beaux cheveux** would mean "I admired lovely hair (i.e., anybody's as long as it was lovely)"; les mains sont propres would give no indication whose hands were clean!

Under this heading, we have one last point to note. When we speak of words like la bouche mouth; la vie, life; le nez, nose, etc., things of which a person has one only, we use the singular of the word in French:

> Je leur ai sauvé la vie. I saved their lives (lit. the life to them).
>
> Ils gardaient le chapeau à la main. They kept their hats in their hands.

Omission of the Article

It is so usual to put in the article, that perhaps it would have been easier to learn when to leave it out. It is often omitted:

In proverbs—

> Pauvreté n'est pas vice. Poverty is no vice.

Before names of streets—

> Il demeure rue Lepic. He lives in Lepic Street.

In rapid enumerations—

> Hommes, femmes, enfants, tous se sauvèrent. Men women, children, all ran away.

There is no article when nouns are used in apposition, i.e., when two nouns referring to the same object are placed next to each other as Londres and capitale are in the next sentence:

> J'arrivai à Londres, capitale de la Grande-Bretagne. I arrived at London, the capital of Great Britain.

"The" is not translated before a comparative:

> Moins il travaille, plus il gagne. The less he works, the more he earns.

With titles too we leave out an article: **la Banque de France,** the Bank of France; **le roi d'Espagne,** the King of Spain. In expressions like **les vins de France,** wines from France, French wines; **des tapis de Perse,** carpets from Persia, Persian carpets, where **de France** and **de Perse** have an adjectival meaning, no article is used. However, we include the article when we refer to a geographical entity: **les richesses de l'Angleterre,** the riches of England (of the whole of England).

With north, south, east and west, usage varies with the points of the compass: talking of winds, we say **le vent du nord, le vent du sud, le vent d'est** and **le vent d'ouest.**

Articles are left out when addressing people: **Bonjour, Docteur,** good morning, doctor, and are generally omitted after the prepositions **par, en, avec, sans** and **de: par avion,** by plane; **en auto,** by car; **avec soin,** with care; **sans exception,** without exception; **un verre de vin,** a glass of wine. No article is needed with expressions like **avoir raison,** to be right; **avoir tort,** to be wrong; **avoir sommeil,** to be sleepy; **faire fortune,** to make a fortune; **vous avez tort comme toujours,** you are wrong as usual; **j'ai sommeil après mon bain,** I'm sleepy after my bathe. With months, days and times too the article is left out: **en avril,** in April; **dimanche prochain,** next Sunday; **à midi, à deux heures,** at noon, at two o'clock.

THE INDEFINITE ARTICLE

	Masc.	Fem.	Meaning
Singular	UN	UNE	A or An
Plural	DES		SOME or ANY

Un journal, a newspaper; **une chose,** a thing; **des chiens,** some dogs.

The Indefinite Article is derived from the Latin numeral

unus, so that it is wise to remember that un or une can also mean "one": une seule chose, one single thing.

Uses of the Indefinite Article

The uses of the Indefinite Article in French and English are very similar. However, it is left out in French in the following cases:

1. When we are describing a person's profession, nationality, rank, religion, etc., together with the verbs être, devenir, élire.

> Elle est Anglaise. She is an Englishwoman.
> Il est docteur. He is a doctor.
> Il a été élu président. He has been elected president.

2. Before the words cent and mille.

> cent hommes, a hundred men.
> mille fois, a thousand times.

3. After quel, sans, ni.

> Quel garçon! what a boy!
> sans argent* ni espoir, without money or hope

4. After par in such phrases as:

> trois fois par jour, three times a day.
> mille francs par semaine, a thousand francs a week.

5. When jamais begins a sentence:

> Jamais écolier ne fut plus heureux que lui. Never was a schoolboy happier than he.

Sometimes, the article is included where in English we should leave it out. We say, just as we do in English: avec courage, avec soin, avec patience, with courage, with care,

---

* In the sentence Il est rentré sans l'argent que vous lui avez donné: He came home without the money that you gave him, the article is included because the noun is particularised. We are not saying that "he returned without money" but that "he returned without the particular money he had been given".

with patience. If we add an adjective the article is used, thus: avec patience, with patience, but avec une grande patience, with great patience; avec soin, with care, but avec une soin minutieux, with minute care. Similarly, un homme de talent, a man of talent, becomes, if supplied with an adjective, un homme d'un talent rare, a man of rare talent.

THE PARTITIVE ARTICLE

Masculine Singular	Feminine Singular	Singular word beginning with a vowel or mute *h*	Plural	Meaning
DU	DE LA	DE L'	DES	*SOME, ANY*

Du pain, some bread; avez-vous de la viande? have you any meat?; il a trouvé de l'or, he found some gold; il y avait des pommiers dans le jardin, there were some apple-trees in the garden.

Use of the Partitive Article

Very similar to English usage, but it should be remembered that the Partitive Article must not be omitted in French, even though it often is in English.

He has money. Il a de l'argent.

There are flowers in the vase. Il y a des fleurs dans le vase.

DE (*or* D' *before a vowel or mute* h) *is used instead of* DU, DE LA, DE L' *or* DES *in the following cases:*

1. After a negative—*

Je n'ai pas de pain. I have not any bread.

* It is possible to use du, de la, de l', des after a negative in a sentence like this: Ce n'est pas du thé, c'est du café. It isn't tea, it's coffee. There is a negative, but it is a negative with a difference. You are not saying that you *haven't anything*. You have *something* but it isn't tea!

Il n'a plus d'argent. He no longer has any money.
Ne buvez pas de vin. Do not drink any wine.
Elle n'a pas de plume.* She hasn't a pen.
Sans casser d'œufs. Without breaking any eggs.
Rien de nouveau. Nothing new.

2. When an adjective comes before a PLURAL NOUN—

de belles choses, some lovely things
d'autres choses, some other things
de bons élèves, some good pupils

[This rule does not apply to a singular noun: du bon tabac, some good tobacco; de la bonne viande, some good meat, or when the adjective comes *after* the noun: des animaux dangereux, some dangerous animals.]

The French do not use this rule when the noun and adjective are used so often together that they have come to be regarded as a single entity: des jeunes filles, some girls; des jeunes gens, youths; des petits pois, peas; des faux pas, mistakes.

---

* "Not a" may also be translated by pas un or pas une (f.), but here the meaning is "not a single one". Thus: "Je n'ai pas un sou." I have not a (single) penny!

CHAPTER III

ADJECTIVES

An adjective is a word used with a noun to give some additional meaning or description. Thus we may say: a good boy, a tall boy, a lazy boy, a fat boy. *Good, tall, lazy, fat* are adjectives describing *boy*.

AGREEMENT OF ADJECTIVES

In French the adjective has several forms: the word "grand" (big) may be spelt, in different circumstances, grand, grande, grands or grandes. The adjective is said to "agree" with its noun, thus if a noun is feminine singular, its adjective must also become feminine singular and add an -e. Similarly, with a masculine plural noun it will generally add an -s, with a feminine plural -es. Perhaps the following examples will make this clearer.

Le garçon est grand.	Masculine Singular
Les garçons sont grands.	Masculine Plural (-s)
La dame est grande.	Feminine Singular (-e)
Les dames sont grandes.	Feminine Plural (-es)

le petit village, the little village; les petits villages, the little villages: la petite ferme, the little farm; les petites fermes, the little farms.

Formation of the Feminine Singular

1. In the majority of cases we add the letter -e to the adjective: grand, grande; petit, petite; ouvert, ouverte.

Le magasin est ouvert. The shop is open.
La fenêtre est ouverte. The window is open.

2. Adjectives which end with an -e in the masculine remain unchanged in the feminine singular. **Jeune** (young);

f. jeune; brave, f. brave; agréable (pleasant), f. agréable: un jeune homme, a young man: une jeune femme, a young woman. [Maître (master) and traître (treacherous) become maîtresse and traîtresse: la carte maîtresse, the master card; la montagne est traîtresse, the mountain is treacherous.]

3. In the case of adjectives ending in -el and -eil [as well as gentil (nice) and nul (no)], the l is doubled before the feminine e. Cruel, f. cruelle; vermeil (vermilion), f. vermeille; gentil, f. gentille; nul, f. nulle. Des lèvres (lips) vermeilles. Une mère cruelle.

(a) Jumeau (twin) becomes jumelle. Des frères jumeaux, twin brothers; des sœurs jumelles, twin sisters.

(b) Beau, beautiful, handsome; nouveau, new; vieux, old; mou, soft; fou, mad, become in the feminine singular belle, nouvelle, vieille, molle, folle.

[Before a masculine singular noun which begins with a vowel or a mute h we use the forms bel, nouvel, vieil, mol, fol.* Un beau garçon, a handsome lad; un bel homme, a handsome man. Une belle femme, a beautiful woman. In the plural the usual masculine plural is used: de beaux garçons, de beaux hommes.

Similarly, le Nouveau Testament, the New Testament; le nouvel an, the new year: un vieil homme, an old man.]

4. Adjectives ending in -en and -on double the n before a feminine e. Bon (good), f. bonne; ancien (old, former), f. ancienne; parisien (Parisian), f. parisienne. Une famille ancienne, an old family.

[Paysan (peasant) becomes paysanne but note bénin (benign), f. bénigne; malin (evil), f. maligne. La maligne influence, the evil influence.]

5. Most adjectives ending in -et double the t [note too sot (foolish), f. sotte]. Muet (dumb), f. muette; net (clean), f. nette.

* When these adjectives come before et (and), one may use either form for the masculine singular: un beau et charmant enfant or un bel et charmant enfant.

Les grandes douleurs sont muettes. Great griefs are the ones not spoken of.

[Complet, complete; concret, concrete; inquiet, anxious; replet, stout; secret, secret; désuet, obsolete become complète, concrète, inquiète, replète, secrète, désuète.]

Idiot becomes idiote. Une réflexion idiote.

6. Bas, low; gras, fat; las, tired; épais, thick; gros, big become basse, grasse, lasse, épaisse, grosse. Une porte basse, a low door. [Other adjectives in -s simply add an e: gris (grey), f. grise, etc.]

7. Faux, false; roux, russet red; exprès, express become fausse, rousse, expresse. Fausses dents, false teeth.

8. Frais, fresh becomes fraîche; favori, favourite becomes favorite. Des fleurs fraîches, fresh flowers; ma couleur favorite, my favourite colour.

9. Adjectives ending in -er change this termination to -ère. Amer, bitter; premier, first become amère, première.

L'onde amère, the bitter sea.

10. Adjectives ending in -x change this letter to -se. Joyeux (joyous), f. joyeuse; jaloux (jealous), f. jalouse. [Doux, sweet, gentle becomes douce.]

11. Adjectives change final -f to -ve in the feminine. Neuf (new), f. neuve; naïf (artless, naive), naïve [bref, brief becomes brève]. Une idée neuve, a new idea.

12. Final -c changes to -que. Public (public), f. publique; turc (Turkish), f. turque. [Note that grec (Greek) becomes grecque.] La langue turque, the Turkish tongue.

13. Blanc, white; franc, frank; sec, dry become blanche, franche, sèche. La race blanche, the white race.

14. Final -g changes to -gue. Long (long), f. longue; oblong (oblong), f. oblongue. Une longue rue: a long street.

15. Final -gu changes to -guë. (The mark is placed over the e to show that the u is to be pronounced. See Diaeresis on page xviii.) Aigu (sharp, acute), f. aiguë; exigu (exiguous), f. exiguë. Une chambre exiguë, a tiny bedroom.

Feminine of Adjectives ending in -EUR

1. Adjectives ending in -eur which are derived from verbs whose stem is also the stem of the present participle, i.e., pêcher, to fish, pêchant, fishing, pêcheur; mentir, to lie, mentant, menteur form their feminine in -euse. Une réponse flatteuse, a flattering reply. [Exceptions are enchanteur, enchanting; pécheur, sinning; vengeur, avenging which become enchanteresse, pécheresse, vengeresse: la femme pécheresse, the woman who was a sinner.]

2. Some adjectives in -teur, not formed from the present participle, change to -trice. Protecteur (protecting), f. protectrice; consolateur (consoling), f. consolatrice. Une épaule protectrice, a protecting shoulder.

3. Ten adjectives, comparative in form and originally at any rate comparative in meaning, simply add an -e. Antérieur, anterior, extérieur, exterior, inférieur, inferior, intérieur, interior, majeur, major, meilleur, better, mineur, minor, postérieur, posterior, supérieur, superior, ultérieur, ulterior. Une meilleure méthode, a better method; la mâchoire inférieure, the lower jaw.

Special Cases

1. Grand does not change in a few hallowed expressions though allied to a feminine; grand'chose, much, a lot; grand'mère, grandmother; grand'messe, high mass; grand' route, highroad; grand'rue, main street, though the apostrophe marks the place where the feminine -e should be found.*

2. Some adjectives have no special feminine form: chic, smart, rococo, rococo, snob, snobbish. Une femme chic, a smart woman; une pendule rococo, a clock in the rococo

* These words may also be spelt without the apostrophe: grand chose, grand mère, grand messe, grand route, grand rue [plurals des grand(s) mères, des grand(s) messes, des grand(s) routes, des grand(s) rues]. To this class belong also grand faim, grand honte, grand soif and grand tante.

style; **maman est un peu snob,** mummy is a little snobbish. Similarly, some adjectives are found only in the feminine: **enceinte,** pregnant.

PLURAL OF ADJECTIVES

The same rules apply to the plural of adjectives as apply to the plural of nouns. All feminine adjectives add -s in the plural: it's only the masculines which give trouble! **Un bon garçon, de bons garçons; un journal loyal, des journaux loyaux; le nouveau bateau, les nouveaux bateaux; un gros tas, de gros tas.**

A few adjectives ending in -al have their masculine plurals in -als: **naval, navals; fatal, fatals; natal, natals; final, finals; banal, banals** (or **banaux**). **Des compliments banals,** banal compliments; **des conseils fatals,** fatal advice.

Adjectives with no Plural Form

Some too have no plural form: **rococo, chic, kaki, sterling.**

Elles ne sont pas chic. They are not smart.
Des uniformes kaki, khaki uniforms.
Cent livres sterling, a hundred pounds sterling.

Tout

Tout, all, every, demands attention. In the masculine plural it loses a *t* and becomes **tous: tous les hommes,** all (the) men. The feminine plural is regular: **toutes les dames.**

Adjective Describing Two or More Nouns

When an adjective refers to several nouns it is put into the plural.

le père et son fils sont charmants. The father and son are charming.

If the nouns are of different genders the adjective is used in the masculine plural form.

> **Madame Dubras et son fils sont charmants.** Mrs. Dubras and her son are charming.

When the adjective has a characteristic feminine form, and the nouns are of different genders, the masculine noun should be placed nearer the adjective.

> **Avec une intonation et un accent parfaits.** With perfect intonation and accent.

Agreement with a Complex Noun

In the case of two nouns joined by **DE**, common sense has to be used to decide with which noun the adjective must agree.

> **Le verre d'eau traditionnel.** The traditional glass of water. (The glass is traditional, not the water.)
>
> **Un régiment d'infanterie complet.** A complete infantry regiment. (The regiment is complete, not the infantry.)
>
> **Un bol de porcelaine blanc (or blanche).** A white porcelain bowl. (The bowl is white and so is the porcelain.)

Avoir l'air

In expressions using "avoir l'air", i.e., to translate sentences like "she looks happy", "she looks sad", etc., one may make the adjective agree either with the subject of the sentence or with the masculine word "l'air".

> She looks cross. **Elle a l'air fâchée (or fâché).**

However, there is a little difference in meaning between the two renderings. **Elle a l'air fâché** means "she *looks* angry", she has an angry look on her face, whereas **elle a l'air fâchée** means "she *seems* angry".

When we are speaking of a thing and not a person the adjective generally agrees with the subject, because a thing cannot change its appearance at will:

> Cette maladie a l'air très sérieuse. This illness seems, looks serious.

If you find this difficult, you can always play safe by inserting d'être and making the adjective agree with the subject.

> Cette chaise a l'air d'être neuve. This chair seems new.

Vous

The polite plural "Vous" referring to one person is, of course, counted as a singular.

> Vous êtes poli, monsieur. You are polite, sir.

But titles like Majesté, Excellence, even when referring to men, are of feminine gender, and therefore require a feminine adjective.

> Votre Majesté a été très bonne. Your Majesty has been most kind.

But add a masculine word and then the adjective will remain masculine.

> Sa majesté le roi est content de vous voir. His Majesty the King is pleased to see you.

Adjectives of Colour

Simple adjectives of colour agree with their noun.

> Il a les cheveux noirs. He has black hair.
> La fleur est blanche. The flower is white.

Compound adjectives of colour are invariable: des yeux bleu clair, light blue eyes; une robe vert pomme, an apple-green dress. A noun used to indicate a colour likewise remains unchanged.

> Des rubans orange. Orange (coloured) ribbons.

Compound Adjectives

(*a*) A compound adjective may consist of two adjectives, both of which qualify the noun. In this case, both parts agree: **des enfants sourds-muets**, deaf and dumb children.*

(*b*) If the compound adjective is made up of an invariable word or of one adjective used as an adverb, only the second part changes.

Des rayons ultra-violets. Ultra-violet rays.
Des personnes haut placées. Highly placed people.

Other examples are **tard-venus**, late comers; **nouveau-nés**, newly born.

[This rule is by no means universal. **Frais, large, grand, bon** agree even when used adverbially: **une rose fraîche cueillie**, a freshly picked rose; **les deux pages grandes ouvertes**, both pages wide open; similarly, **raide-mort**, stone-dead; **ivre-mort**, dead-drunk, become **raides-morts, ivres-morts** in the masculine plural.]

Demi (half)

When **demi** is used before a noun to which it is attached by a hyphen it is invariable: **une demi-heure**, half an hour; **elle est demi-morte**, she is half dead. Placed after a noun, **demi** agrees: **trois heures et demie**, half-past three. **Mi** (half) is always invariable and does not exist except when joined to a word by a hyphen: **la mi-janvier**, mid January; **la mi-été**, midsummer; **la mi-temps**, half-time (in these cases the compound is feminine); **les yeux mi-clos**, eyes half-closed.

Excepté

Excepté, except; **ci-joint**, enclosed; **y compris**, including; **franc de port**, post-free, remain invariable when placed

---

* However, one says, **une fille mort-née**, a still-born daughter, without making **mort** feminine, though the child is both born and dead.

before a noun or pronoun: excepté elle, except for her; ci-joint sa lettre, her letter is enclosed; y compris la France, including France. Like demi, when placed after a noun they agree.

Feu * (late, deceased)

Feu, used in the singular only, agrees if it is preceded by an article or possessive adjective. Thus feu la reine or la feue reine, the late queen; feu mes oncles, my deceased uncles; ma feue sœur, my late sister.

Haut (high), bas (low)

Haut and bas are used adverbially in expressions like haut les mains! up with your hands! bas les pattes! down with your paws! and so do not agree.

Nu (bare, naked)

Nu used before a noun is invariable and is joined to it by a hyphen: nu-jambes, bare-legged; nu-pieds, bare-footed; nu-bras, bare-armed. After the noun, it agrees: la tête nue, bare-headed; marcher pieds nus, to walk bare-footed.

Possible

Possible does not change in expressions using le plus, le moins.

> Courez le moins de risques possible. Run the fewest risks possible.

Adjectives Used as Adverbs

In expressions like voler bas, to fly low; sentir bon, to smell good; marcher droit, to walk straight; couper court,

---

* Feu is used only in the literary language. Otherwise one says mon défunt père, my late father, ma défunte mère, my deceased mother.

to cut short; **chanter faux**, to sing out of tune; **parler haut**, to speak up, the adjectives **bas**, **bon**, **droit**, etc., are used as adverbs, and therefore do not agree.

> **les cheveux coupés court**, hair cut short
> **Cette viande sent bon.** That meat smells good.

POSITION OF THE ADJECTIVE

The general rule is that the adjective follows its noun: **la langue française**, the French language; **la maison blanche**, the white house; **la table ronde**, the round table.

However, the adjective may come in front of the noun when both are considered as a single idea, a single unit of thought: **la jeune fille**, the girl; **le petit pois**, the pea; **un jeune homme**, a youth; **un petit chien**, a pup.

These rules have numerous exceptions, especially in the literary language, where for purposes of style all kinds of variations of usage are possible.

Put the Adjective before the Noun

1. When the adjective is a short and common one, and especially when the noun has several syllables: **un petit appartement**, a small flat; **un long voyage**, a long journey. Other adjectives which generally precede are **grand**, big, tall; **gros**, big; **haut**, high; **beau**, beautiful; **joli**, pretty; **vilain**, ugly; **jeune**, young; **vieux**, old; **court**, short; **bon**, good, kind; **mauvais**, bad.

2. When the adjective is considered as the usual and fitting one: **le brave soldat**, the brave soldier; **la verte Irlande**, green Ireland; **la douce mère**, the sweet mother; **la terrible catastrophe**, the terrible catastrophe; **votre charmante sœur**, your charming sister.

Put the Adjective after the Noun

1. When the adjective is a long one, especially if the noun is monosyllabic: **un chant harmonieux**, a sweet song.

2. When it is an adjective of colour or shape: **un champ oblong**, an oblong field; **une robe noire**, a black dress.

3. If it is an adjective of nationality: **un livre français**, a French book.

4. If the adjective is followed by a phrase: **une chambre grande comme la main**, a bedroom as big as your hand.

5. When you are in doubt. (Most adjectives follow the noun!)

Adjectives Which Vary in Meaning According to their Position

Some adjectives vary in meaning when they are put before or after a noun. Here are some examples:

Before	*After*
un ancien élève, a former pupil	une maison ancienne, an old house
un brave homme, a worthy man	un homme brave, a brave man
ma chère femme, my beloved wife	une robe chère, an expensive dress
le dernier jour de la semaine, the last day of the week (last of a series)	mercredi dernier, last Wednesday (the one that's just gone)
un grand homme, a great man	un homme grand, a tall man
une pauvre femme, an unfortunate woman	une femme pauvre, a poor (without money) woman
ma propre main, my own hand	les mains propres, clean hands
la seule chose, the only thing	une femme seule, a woman on her own
une triste affaire, a wretched business	une journée triste, a sorrowful day

Nouveau and Neuf

Both mean "new", but **neuf** is used with the sense of "brand-new", "fresh from the shop", "just made".

Ma nouvelle voiture n'est pas neuve. My new car is not a brand-new one.

Two or More Adjectives with the Same Noun

This requires care. If one adjective normally comes before, the other after, there is no problem: **une petite table ronde**, a little round table. When the adjective and noun are linked closely—**une petite fille**, a little girl—you may add another in its normal position: **une jolie petite fille**, a pretty little girl; **une petite fille intelligente**, a clever little girl. In most cases you join the two adjectives together by **et** and for preference put them after the noun: **une table longue et basse**, a long, low table.

Position of Adjective with a Complex Noun

When we have a complex noun like **hôtel de ville**, town hall; **cahier d'écolier**, (schoolboys') exercise book, the adjective is put in its usual place: **un bel hôtel de ville**, a fine town hall; **un cahier d'écolier vert**, a green exercise book. When, however, there would be ambiguity, the adjective is not placed after the second noun: **un sale cahier d'écolier**, a dirty exercise book (it's the book, and not the schoolboy, which is dirty!).

POSSESSIVE ADJECTIVES

Possessive adjectives, as their name implies, are attached to a word to show ownership: *my* book, *thy* book, *his* book, *her* book, *our* book, *your* book, *their* book.

Meaning	Before Masculine Singular Nouns	Before Feminine Singular Nouns	Before Plural Nouns
my	mon	ma	mes
thy	ton	ta	tes
his, her, its, one's	son	sa	ses
our	notre	notre	nos
your	votre	votre	vos
their	leur	leur	leurs

Examples: ma pomme, my apple; son livre, his or her book; sa mère, his or her mother; nos plumes, our pens; leurs chapeaux, their hats; le ciel et sa beauté, the sky and its beauty; on aime sa patrie, one loves one's country.

Use of the Possessive Adjectives

1. *His* or *her*; translated by the same word in French. Son or sa depend on the gender of the *noun*, not of the *possessor*: son livre, his or her book; sa mère, his or her mother. If you are really afraid of not making yourself perfectly clear, say sa mère à lui, *his* mother; sa mère à elle, *her* mother.

2. Mon, ton, son are used instead of ma, ta, sa if a feminine singular word begins with a vowel or mute h: mon encre (f.), my ink; ton auto (f.), thy car; son âme (f.), his or her soul; son inoubliable histoire (f.), his, her or its unforgettable story.

3. In English the possessive adjective may be understood and therefore omitted: in French it must be repeated: his pen and book, sa plume et son livre; my brother and sister, mon frère et ma sœur.

4. A soldier * speaking to an upper rank always says **mon lieutenant, mon capitaine, mon général** when spoken to by an officer.

5. When an owner possesses only one of the objects, the singular of the adjective and noun is generally used.

> **Les oiseaux font leur nid au printemps.** Birds make their nests in spring.
>
> **Ils ôtèrent leur chapeau.** They removed their hats.

If, however, there is an insistence on the number or variety, then the plural is used:

> **Les marchands ouvrent leurs boutiques aujourd'hui.** Shopkeepers open their shops today.

Sometimes too it is essential to use the plural to avoid producing a ludicrous effect:

> **L'après-midi les messieurs se promenaient avec leurs femmes.** In the afternoon the gentlemen used to walk with their wives.

(The singular "femme" might imply a society in which the gentlemen shared a wife!)

6. As already pointed out in Chapter II, the possessive adjective is replaced by the Definite Article when there is no doubt about the identity of the possessor, especially where parts of the body are concerned.

> **Il leva la tête.** He raised his head.
>
> **On lui attacha les pieds.** One tied his feet (lit. the feet to him).

Of course, the possessive adjective is allowed when some additional emphasis is required:

> **Il a toujours sa grippe.** He still has his influenza (that influenza of his).
>
> **Tes beaux yeux!** Your lovely eyes!

---

* A civilian would say simply **monsieur** or **lieutenant**, etc.

DEMONSTRATIVE ADJECTIVES

Demonstrative Adjectives are used to point out the nouns with which they are associated.

	Masculine	Feminine	Meaning
Singular	ce or cet	cette	this *or* that
Plural	ces		these *or* those

Examples: **ce crayon,** this pencil, that pencil; **cet homme,** this man, that man; **cette maison,** this house, that house; **ces amis,** these friends, those friends.

In the masculine *singular*, **cet** is used before a vowel or mute h: **cet ami,** this friend; **cet autre livre,** this other book; **cet homme,** this man.

This adjective may be reinforced by placing the particles **-ci** or **-là** after the noun:

-ci (here) gives the idea of nearness: **ce livre-ci,** *this* book.
-là (there) gives the impression of distance: **ce livre-là,** *that* book.

Voulez-vous cette chambre-ci ou cette chambre-là? Do you want *this* bedroom or *that* bedroom?

INTERROGATIVE ADJECTIVES

1. **Quel?** (which?, what?). The interrogative adjective **quel** (which? *or* what?) has four forms in French: **quel,** masculine singular, **quelle,** feminine singular, **quels,** masculine plural, **quelles,** feminine plural.

Quel livre désirez-vous? Which book do you want?
Quelle femme est là? Which woman is there?
Quelle est cette odeur agréable? What is that pleasant smell?

De quelle couleur est cette robe? What colour is this dress?

Quelle heure est-il? What time is it?

2. Quel! (what a!, what!). This adjective may also be used to indicate astonishment.

Quel chien! What a dog!
Quelle ville! What a town!
Quels élèves! What pupils!

Notice the absence of the article "a" in the above examples.

3. Quel may also be used with the subjunctive in clauses like these:

Quel que soit votre avis . . . Whatever may be your opinion . . .

Quelle que soit la maladie . . . Whatever the illness may be . . .

Quelles que soient vos raisons . . . Whatever your reasons may be . . .

4. Quel is also used in conjunction with n'importe and je ne sais:

Achetez n'importe quel journal! Buy any paper you please! (No matter which.)

Il est sorti pour je ne sais quelle raison. He went out for some reason or other. (I don't know what.)

INDEFINITE ADJECTIVES

Here is a list of some indefinite adjectives with examples of their uses:

aucun, nul, no, not any

Il n'a donné $\left\{\begin{matrix} \text{aucune} \\ \text{nulle} \end{matrix}\right\}$ raison. He gave no reason.

sans aucune protection, without any protection

autre, other

> **un autre jour,** another day
> **d'autres livres,** other books
> **les autres tables,** the other tables
> **Il n'est pas comme les autres.** He isn't like the others (the rest).
> **nous autres Anglais,** we English people
> **Il y a autre chose.** There's something else.
> **Avez-vous autre chose à me montrer?** Have you anything else to show me?

certain, certain

> **un certain homme,** a certain man
> **une chose certaine,** a sure thing
> **la mort certaine,** certain, sure death
> **Certains l'ont déjà dit.** Certain people have already said so.

chaque, each, every

> **Chaque jour il fait la même chose.** Every day he does the same thing.
> **Chaque fois qu'il y entre** . . . Every time he goes in . . .

même, same, very, self

> **la même chose,** the same thing
> **le même prix,** the same price
> **Les officiers mêmes refusèrent d'obéir.** The very officers refused to obey.
> **Ma sœur est la bonté même.** My sister is kindness itself.
> **Je le ferai, moi-même.** I shall do it myself.

When même is used in front of the article and a noun, it is invariable.

> **Même les chiens refusent de manger cela.** Even the dogs refuse to eat that.

It does not change if used similarly before an adjective or a verb.

Ils sont bons et même indulgents. They are kind and
even indulgent.

Ils veulent même venir avec nous. They even want to
come with us.

plusieurs, several

plusieurs enfants, several children
plusieurs femmes, several women

quelque(s), some, a few

quelque chose de nouveau, something new
quelque part, somewhere
quelques fleurs, a few flowers

quelconque, some or other

une idée quelconque, some idea or other
un livre quelconque (familiar style), a very ordinary
kind of book

tel, such

un tel garçon, such a boy
une telle chose, such a thing
de tels livres, such books
Telle fut sa patience que . . . Such was her patience
that . . .
Telle qu'elle est, je l'aime. I love her just as she is.
Monsieur un Tel, Mr. So-and-so

tout, toute, every, all (sing.)

tous, toutes, all (plur.)

tout ceci, all this
tout le jour, all day, the whole day
toute ma famille, all my family, the whole of my family
tous les jours, every day
tous les deux jours, every other day
tous (les) deux, both
tous trois, all three

Tout homme bien élevé aurait fait la même chose.

$\left.\begin{array}{l}\text{Any}\\\text{Every}\end{array}\right\}$ well-brought-up man would have done the same thing.

COMPARISON OF ADJECTIVES

Adjectives are said to have degrees of comparison: positive, comparative and superlative. If we take a common adjective like "high", then we can say "high" (positive), "higher" (comparative), "highest" (superlative). With longer adjectives we do not use this method: instead we employ "more" and "most": thus, "beautiful" (positive), "more beautiful" (comparative), "most beautiful" (superlative). This latter method is the French way of doing it,

Positive	Comparative	Superlative
haut (high)	plus haut (higher)	le plus haut (highest)
confortable (comfortable)	plus confortable (more comfortable)	le plus confortable (most comfortable)
long (long)	plus long (longer)	le plus long (longest)

and is used for most French adjectives.

Exceptions

In English we have a few exceptions like "good, better, best", "bad, worse, worst". Here are the exceptions in French:

bon (good)	meilleur (better)	le meilleur (best)
mauvais (bad)	pire (worse)	le pire (worst)
petit (little)	moindre (less, lesser)	le moindre (least)

Mauvais and petit can also be compared with plus, thus:

mauvais	plus mauvais	le plus mauvais
petit (small)	plus petit (smaller)	le plus petit (smallest)

There is a slight difference in meaning between the two forms. For instance, le plus petit stands for the smallest in size.

De tous les enfants, c'est Jean qui est le plus petit. Jean is the smallest of the children.

Le moindre has the sense of "the slightest", and is used with abstract nouns.

Il l'a fait sans la moindre difficulté. He did it without the slightest difficulty.

Similarly, le plus mauvais means "worst" in a concrete sense: les plus mauvais souliers, les plus mauvais habits, the worst shoes, the worst clothes, whereas le pire means "worst" referring to moral matters: la pire corruption, the worst corruption.

Examples of Comparison

Now let us have a few examples of comparison:

Jean est grand. Jean is tall.

Jean est plus grand que son frère. Jean is taller than his brother.

Jean est le plus grand garçon de la classe. Jean is the tallest boy in the class.

Note that "than" is expressed by que and that whereas in English we say "in" after a superlative, "the tallest boy *in* the class, the prettiest house *in* the street, the best restaurant *in* Paris", the French always use de, "of the class, of the street, of Paris".

Suzanne est aussi grande que Pierre. Suzanne is as tall as Pierre.

Suzanne n'est pas ${si \atop aussi}$ } grande que Pierre. Suzanne is not ${so \atop as}$ } tall as Pierre.

Suzanne est moins grande que Pierre. Suzanne is less tall than } not so tall as } Pierre.

Note the use of **que** in all the above examples.

> **Suzanne est le moins beau de mes enfants.** Suzanne is the least beautiful of my children.

Thus, using **moins** (less), and **le moins** (least), we can make unflattering comparisons: **confortable** (comfortable), **moins confortable** (less comfortable), **le moins confortable** (least comfortable).

The position of the adjective need not worry you: it goes into its normal place, either before or after the noun: **Le plus beau tableau du musée**, the most beautiful picture in the museum; **le garçon le plus intelligent**, the most intelligent boy; **les exercices les plus difficiles**, the most difficult exercises.

When a possessive adjective is used with a superlative and the adjective is one which precedes the noun the article is omitted: **ma plus belle photo**, my finest photo, *but* **mes livres les plus intéressants**, my most interesting books.

Most

There is also a use of "most" which is not really a direct comparison. We say "he is a most charming gentleman", meaning "he is exceedingly charming" and without consciously comparing him with anyone else. In this case we should translate by **un monsieur des plus charmants** or **un monsieur très charmant**: similarly, **un livre des plus intéressants**, a most interesting book. We could also say: **un livre fort intéressant** or **un livre bien intéressant**, a very interesting book, which amounts more or less to the same thing.

Other phrases worth learning are **de plus en plus**, more and more; **de moins en moins**, less and less: **de plus en plus sérieux**, more and more serious; **de plus en plus grand**, bigger and bigger; **de moins en moins important**, less and less important.

Comme

There remains yet another way of comparing, using comme: **fort comme un âne**, as strong as an ass (strong like an ass); **doux comme un agneau**, as gentle as a lamb.

You will have noticed already that when a definite article is used there is no difference in form between a comparative and a superlative adjective, thus: **fort**, strong; **plus fort**, stronger; **le plus fort**, the stronger. **Le plus fort** may, as we have already seen, also mean "the strongest". Now look at these two sentences:

Jacques is the stronger (of my two sons).
Jacques is the strongest (of my three sons).

In both cases, the sentences would begin in French:

Jacques est le plus fort . . .

Expletive NE in Comparison

One last point. In sentences like "He is stronger than you think" and "He talks more than he works", the comparative is followed in the **que** clause by an untranslated or expletive **ne**.

Il est plus fort que vous ne pensez.
Il parle plus qu'il ne travaille.

CARDINAL NUMBERS

0	zéro	9	neuf
1	un (m.), une (f.)	10	dix
2	deux	11	onze
3	trois	12	douze
4	quatre	13	treize
5	cinq	14	quatorze
6	six	15	quinze
7	sept	16	seize
8	huit	17	dix-sept

18	dix-huit	60	soixante
19	dix-neuf	61	soixante et un
20	vingt	66	soixante-six
21	vingt et un	70	soixante-dix
22	vingt-deux	71	soixante et onze
23	vingt-trois	72	soixante-douze
24	vingt-quatre	73	soixante-treize
25	vingt-cinq	74	soixante-quatorze
26	vingt-six	75	soixante-quinze
27	vingt-sept	76	soixante-seize
28	vingt-huit	77	soixante-dix-sept
29	vingt-neuf	78	soixante-dix-huit
30	trente	79	soixante-dix-neuf
31	trente et un	80	quatre-vingts
32	trente-deux	81	quatre-vingt-un
40	quarante	82	quatre-vingt-deux
41	quarante et un	83	quatre-vingt-trois
43	quarante-trois	84	quatre-vingt-quatre
50	cinquante	90	quatre-vingt-dix
51	cinquante et un	91	quatre-vingt-onze
55	cinquante-cinq	92	quatre-vingt-douze

100	cent
101	cent un
102	cent deux
200	deux cents
201	deux cent un
1000	mille
1001	mille un
2000	deux mille
1,000,000	un million
2,000,000	deux millions
1,000,000,000	un milliard

Uses of Cardinal Numbers

Cardinal numbers may be simple, un, deux, trois or compound, dix-sept, vingt et un, quatre-vingt-treize. French compound numbers from 17 to 99 inclusive have hyphens between their component parts except when et is used as a joining word: 21, 31, 41, 51, 61, 71; vingt et un, trente et un, quarante et un, etc. After 71 no et is used: quatre-vingt-un (81), quatre-vingt-onze (91), cent un (101). Vingt and cent take an -s when multiplied by another number:* quatre-vingts (80), quatre cents (400), but not if another number follows: quatre-vingt-trois (83), quatre cent dix (410). The only number which has a feminine form is UN, so that we say une maison, one house; vingt et une maisons, twenty-one houses. Mille, a thousand, has no plural form: trois mille hommes, three thousand men. Million and milliard are nouns, and therefore we must say trois millions de francs (3,000,000 francs) and un milliard de livres (£1,000,000,000). Cardinal numbers are used (with the exception of premier, first) with names of kings and in dates: Louis premier, Louis I, but Louis deux, Louis II, Louis trois, Louis III, etc., le premier décembre, December 1st, but le deux décembre, le trois décembre, etc.

Cardinal numbers are generally placed before the noun, trois sacs, three bags: they come afterwards to indicate the order of kings, popes, etc., Louis quatorze, Louis XIV, and to give a reference, chapitre cinq, chapter five.

ORDINAL NUMBERS

1st	premier (m.), première (f.)	6th	sixième
2nd	deuxième, second(e)	7th	septième
3rd	troisième	8th	huitième
4th	quatrième	9th	neuvième
5th	cinquième	10th	dixième
	21st	vingt et unième	
	33rd	trente-troisième	

* In expressions like page deux cent, page quatre-vingt, where the number follows the noun, no -s is required.

Use, Formation and Position of Ordinals

They indicate order: le premier homme, the first man; le cinquième jour, the fifth day; il est arrivé le septième, he came in seventh. They are formed, with the exception of premier, from the cardinal numbers by the addition of -ième. Of course, with numbers ending in -e, like quatre, quatorze, quarante, the e is dropped before the ending: quatrième, quatorzième, quarantième. Note too that cinq adds a u to become cinquième and that the f of neuf becomes a v in neuvième.

There are two words for second: deuxième and second (pronounced *zegond*). In compound numbers we always use deuxième; vingt-deuxième, twenty-second. In other cases either deuxième or second may be used: le deuxième livre, le second livre.* Deuxième seems to be more common than second.

Ordinal adjectives come before the noun and, of course, agree like normal adjectives: ma première auto, my first car.

* It used to be stated that, when speaking of two things only, second should be used, of more than two, deuxième was better.

CHAPTER IV

THE VERB

TENSES AND PERSONS

The verb is the most important word in the sentence: it expresses the action that takes place. Unfortunately it is also the most difficult word to use correctly. A verb is generally found in tenses, which give evidence of the occasion when the action takes place, whether in the past, the present or the future. Each tense has six forms, 1st, 2nd and 3rd Persons Singular and 1st, 2nd and 3rd Persons Plural. Thus the Present Tense of the verb "to like" can be written down thus in English:

	Singular	*Plural*
1st Person	I like	we like
2nd Person	thou likest	you like
3rd Person	he, she, it likes	they like

This in French would be written like this:

1st Person	j'aime	nous aimons
2nd Person	tu aimes	vous aimez
3rd Person	il, elle aime	ils, elles aiment

TU

The 2nd Person Singular form **Tu** (thou), which has almost died out in English, is very common in French, being used when members of a family are speaking to each other, in conversation between close friends and when calling animals. In prayer, Catholics and Protestants both use **Tu** (Thou), the familiar form of 'you'.

MOODS

The Verb has also Moods: the Indicative Mood, the Conditional Mood, the Imperative, the Subjunctive and the Infinitive Moods.

Tenses of the Indicative Mood

Here are the four simple tenses of the Indicative of the verb donner (to give) with their equivalents in English:

Present Tense: **je donne,** I give, I am giving, I do give
Imperfect Tense: **je donnais,** I was giving, I used to give
Past Historic Tense: **je donnai,** I gave, I did give
Future Tense: **je donnerai,** I shall give

Compound Tenses

In addition to these four simple tenses, there are four compound tenses (i.e., where the verb is made up of two parts).

Perfect Tense: **j'ai donné,** I have given, I gave
Pluperfect Tense: **j'avais donné,** I had given
Past Anterior Tense: **j'eus donné,** I had given
Future Perfect Tense: **j'aurai donné,** I shall have given

Conditional Mood

The Conditional Mood has two tenses only:

Conditional Tense: **je donnerais,** I should give
Conditional Perfect Tense: **j'aurais donné,** I should have given

Imperative Mood

The Imperative Mood is used to give commands.

2nd Person Singular: **donne!** give!
1st Person Plural: **donnons!** let us give!
2nd Person Plural: **donnez!** give!

The Subjunctive Mood

The Subjunctive has four tenses whose meanings are generally the same as the corresponding tenses of the Indicative.

Present Tense: je donne
Imperfect Tense: je donnasse
Perfect Tense: j'aie donné
Pluperfect Tense: j'eusse donné

The Infinitive

The Infinitive has two forms:

Present Infinitive: donner, to give
Perfect Infinitive: avoir donné, to have given

Participles

Present Participle: donnant, giving
Past Participle: donné, given

Active and Passive Voice

Every tense can be in the active voice or in the passive voice. Here are two examples:

Present Tense (Active Voice): je punis, I punish
Present Tense (Passive Voice): je suis puni, I am punished
Future Tense (Active Voice): je punirai, I shall punish
Future Tense (Passive Voice): je serai puni, I shall be punished

After the above preliminaries, let us go into more detail. There are thousands of French verbs, and learning them thoroughly is a task which every student must tackle boldly. To make things easier, it is usual to divide verbs into families or conjugations. Here is the usual classification:

CONJUGATIONS

1. The first conjugation: Verbs ending in -ER, like donner, to give.

2. The second conjugation: Verbs ending in -IR, like finir, to finish.

3. The third conjugation: Verbs ending in -RE, like vendre, to sell.

There remain the Irregular Verbs which, as their name implies, do not always behave like the verbs of the three conjugations. A list of these verbs is given later in this chapter.

THE FIRST CONJUGATION

Verbs whose Infinitive ends in -ER.

This conjugation is by far the most important, containing over four thousand verbs. Moreover, any new verb brought into the language—kidnapper, to kidnap; interviewer, to interview—goes into this category.

Donner, to give

Indicative Mood

Present Tense.

je donne, I give, am giving, do give
tu donnes, thou givest, etc.
il (elle) donne, he (she) gives, etc.
nous donnons, we give, etc.

vous donnez, you give, etc.
ils (elles) donnent, they give, etc.

Imperfect Tense.

je donnais, I was giving, used to give
tu donnais, thou wast giving, etc.
il donnait, he was giving, etc.
nous donnions, we were giving, etc.
vous donniez, you were giving, etc.
ils donnaient, they were giving, etc.

Past Historic.

je donnai, I gave, I did give
tu donnas, thou gavest, etc.
il donna, he gave, etc.
nous donnâmes, we gave, etc.
vous donnâtes, you gave, etc.
ils donnèrent, they gave, etc.

Future.

je donnerai, I shall give
tu donneras, thou wilt give
il donnera, he will give
nous donnerons, we shall give
vous donnerez, you will give
ils donneront, they will give

Compound Tenses

Perfect.	Pluperfect.
j'ai donné, I have given, I gave	j'avais donné, I had given
tu as donné, thou hast given, etc.	tu avais donné, thou hadst given
il a donné, he has given, etc.	il avait donné, he had given
nous avons donné, we have given, etc.	nous avions donné, we had given
vous avez donné, you have given, etc.	vous aviez donné, you had given
ils ont donné, they have given, etc.	ils avaient donné, they had given

Past Anterior.	Future Perfect.
j'eus donné, I had given	j'aurai donné, I shall have given
tu eus donné, thou hadst given	tu auras donné, thou wilt have given
il eut donné, he had given	il aura donné, he will have given
nous eûmes donné, we had given	nous aurons donné, we shall have given
vous eûtes donné, you had given	vous aurez donné, you will have given
ils eurent donné, they had given	ils auront donné, they will have given

Conditional Mood

Conditional.	Conditional Perfect.
je donnerais, I should give	j'aurais donné, I should have given
tu donnerais, thou wouldst give	tu aurais donné, thou wouldst have given
il donnerait, he would give	il aurait donné, he would have given
nous donnerions, we should give	nous aurions donné, we should have given
vous donneriez, you would give	vous auriez donné, you would have given
ils donneraient, they would give	ils auraient donné, they would have given

Subjunctive Mood

Present.	Imperfect.
je donne	je donnasse
tu donnes	tu donnasses
il donne	il donnât
nous donnions	nous donnassions
vous donniez	vous donnassiez
ils donnent	ils donnassent

Perfect.	Pluperfect.
j'aie donné	j'eusse donné
tu aies donné	tu eusses donné
il ait donné	il eût donné
nous ayons donné	nous eussions donné
vous ayez donné	vous eussiez donné
ils aient donné	ils eussent donné

Imperative Mood

Affirmative.	Negative.
donne! give (thou)!	ne donne pas! do not give!
donnons! let us give!	ne donnons pas! let us not give!
donnez! give (you)!	ne donnez pas! do not give!

Infinitive Mood

Present.	Past.
donner, to give	avoir donné, to have given

Participles

Present.	Past.
donnant, giving	donné, given
	ayant donné, having given

All verbs ending in -ER, with the exceptions of aller and envoyer, are like donner.

Minor Peculiarities of the First Conjugation

A few verbs ending in -ER, while not irregular, have a few minor peculiarities. We shall deal with these now.

Verbs Ending in -CER

Examples: commencer, to commence; lancer, to throw.
Verbs ending in -CER have a cedilla under the c before a and o in order to keep the same soft c sound.

commencer   nous commençons   je commençais

Verbs Ending in -GER

These add a mute or silent e before endings that begin with a and o in order to keep the soft g sound.

manger	nous mangeons	ils mangeaient
plonger	nous plongeons	il plongeait

Verbs Ending in -YER

These change the y to i before a mute or silent e.*

essayer	il essaie	nous essaierons
broyer	je broie	tu broieras
essuyer	ils essuient	ils essuieront

Verbs Like RÉGNER, CÉDER, PROTÉGER

These change the é to è before a mute e in the endings of the Present Tense.

cĕder: je cède but vous cédez
pénétrer: ils pénètrent but nous pénétrons

In the Future and Conditional Tenses the accents are not changed: je céderai, il protégerait, ils céderaient.

Verbs Like SEMER, LEVER, PROMENER, ACHETER, GELER

These verbs take a grave accent over the e when there is a mute e following: semer, je sème; lever, ils lèvent; promener, je promènerai; acheter, elle achètera; geler, il gèle.

Other Verbs Ending in -ELER and -ETER

These double the l or t in similar circumstances: jeter, ils jettent; appeler, j'appellerai but vous appelez.

* Verbs ending in ayer, i.e., payer, may either keep the y or change it to i: payer, je paye or je paie.

SECOND AND THIRD CONJUGATIONS
(Verbs ending in -IR and -RE)

There are far fewer verbs ending in -IR and only a small number ending in -RE.

Second Conjugation
FINIR, to finish

Third Conjugation
VENDRE, to sell

Indicative Mood

Present. *I finish*	Imperfect. *{ I was finishing* *{ I used to finish*	Present. *I sell*	Imperfect. *{ I was selling* *{ I used to sell*
je finis	je finissais	je vends	je vendais
tu finis	tu finissais	tu vends	tu vendais
il finit	il finissait	il vend	il vendait
nous finissons	nous finissions	nous vendons	nous vendions
vous finissez	vous finissiez	vous vendez	vous vendiez
ils finissent	ils finissaient	ils vendent	ils vendaient

Past Historic. *I finished*	Future. *I shall finish*	Past Historic. *I sold*	Future. *I shall sell*
je finis	je finirai	je vendis	je vendrai
tu finis	tu finiras	tu vendis	tu vendras
il finit	il finira	il vendit	il vendra
nous finîmes	nous finirons	nous vendîmes	nous vendrons
vous finîtes	vous finirez	vous vendîtes	vous vendrez
ils finirent	ils finiront	ils vendirent	ils vendront

Compound Tenses

Perfect. *I have finished*	Pluperfect. *I had finished*	Perfect. *I have sold*	Pluperfect. *I had sold*
j'ai fini	j'avais fini	j'ai vendu	j'avais vendu
tu as fini	tu avais fini	tu as vendu	tu avais vendu
il a fini	il avait fini	il a vendu	il avait vendu
nous avons fini	nous avions fini	nous avons vendu	nous avions vendu
vous avez fini	vous aviez fini	vous avez vendu	vous aviez vendu
ils ont fini	ils avaient fini	ils ont vendu	ils avaient vendu

Conditional Mood

Conditional.	Conditional Perfect.	Conditional.	Conditional Perfect.
I should finish	*I should have finished*	*I should sell*	*I should have sold*
je finirais	j'aurais fini	je vendrais	j'aurais vendu
tu finirais	tu aurais fini	tu vendrais	tu aurais vendu
il finirait	il aurait fini	il vendrait	il aurait vendu
nous finirions	nous aurions fini	nous vendrions	nous aurions vendu
vous finiriez	vous auriez fini	vous vendriez	vous auriez vendu
ils finiraient	ils auraient fini	ils vendraient	ils auraient vendu

Subjunctive Mood

Present.	Imperfect.	Present.	Imperfect.
je finisse	je finisse	je vende	je vendisse
tu finisses	tu finisses	tu vendes	tu vendisses
il finisse	il finît	il vende	il vendît
nous finissions	nous finissions	nous vendions	nous vendissions
vous finissiez	vous finissiez	vous vendiez	vous vendissiez
ils finissent	ils finissent	ils vendent	ils vendissent

Perfect.	Pluperfect.	Perfect.	Pluperfect.
j'aie fini	j'eusse fini	j'aie vendu	j'eusse vendu
tu aies fini	tu eusses fini	tu aies vendu	tu eusses vendu
il ait fini	il eût fini	il ait vendu	il eût vendu
nous ayons fini	nous eussions fini	nous ayons vendu	nous eussions vendu
vous ayez fini	vous eussiez fini	vous ayez vendu	vous eussiez vendu
ils aient fini	ils eussent fini	ils aient vendu	ils eussent vendu

Imperative Mood

finis! finish (thou)!	vends! sell (thou)!
finissons! let us finish!	vendons! let us sell!
finissez! finish!	vendez! sell!

Infinitive

Present: finir, to finish	vendre, to sell
Perfect: avoir fini, to have finished	avoir vendu, to have sold

Participles

Present: finissant, finishing	vendant, selling
Past: fini, finished	vendu, sold
ayant fini, having finished	ayant vendu, having sold

AVOIR and ÊTRE

You will have noticed that in the Compound Tenses another verb, avoir, is brought in to help. There are two such auxiliary verbs: avoir, to have, and être, to be. We must look at them at once.

Avoir, to have   Être, to be

Indicative Mood

Present.	Imperfect.	Present.	Imperfect.
I have	*I had* *I was having* *I used to have*	*I am*	*I was* *I used to be*
j'ai	j'avais	je suis	j'étais
tu as	tu avais	tu es	tu étais
il a	il avait	il est	il était
nous avons	nous avions	nous sommes	nous étions
vous avez	vous aviez	vous êtes	vous étiez
ils ont	ils avaient	ils sont	ils étaient

Past Historic.	Future.	Past Historic.	Future.
I had	*I shall have*	*I was*	*I shall be*
j'eus	j'aurai	je fus	je serai
tu eus	tu auras	tu fus	tu seras
il eut	il aura	il fut	il sera
nous eûmes	nous aurons	nous fûmes	nous serons
vous eûtes	vous aurez	vous fûtes	vous serez
ils eurent	ils auront	ils furent	ils seront

Compound Tenses

Perfect.	Pluperfect.	Perfect.	Pluperfect.
I have had	*I had had*	*I have been*	*I had been*
j'ai eu	j'avais eu	j'ai été	j'avais été
tu as eu	tu avais eu	tu as été	tu avais été
il a eu	il avait eu	il a été	il avait été
nous avons eu	nous avions eu	nous avons été	nous avions été
vous avez eu	vous aviez eu	vous avez été	vous aviez été
ils ont eu	ils avaient eu	ils ont été	ils avaient été

Past Anterior.	Future Perfect.	Past Anterior.	Future Perfect.
I had had	*I shall have had*	*I had been*	*I shall have been*
j'eus eu	j'aurai eu	j'eus été	j'aurai été
tu eus eu	tu auras eu	tu eus été	tu auras été
il eut eu	il aura eu	il eut été	il aura été
nous eûmes eu	nous aurons eu	nous eûmes été	nous aurons été
vous eûtes eu	vous aurez eu	vous eûtes été	vous aurez été
ils eurent eu	ils auront eu	ils eurent été	ils auront été

Conditional Mood

Conditional.	Conditional Perfect.	Conditional.	Conditional Perfect.
I should have	*I should have had*	*I should be*	*I should have been*
j'aurais	j'aurais eu	je serais	j'aurais été
tu aurais	tu aurais eu	tu serais	tu aurais été
il aurait	il aurait eu	il serait	il aurait été
nous aurions	nous aurions eu	nous serions	nous aurions été
vous auriez	vous auriez eu	vous seriez	vous auriez été
ils auraient	ils auraient eu	ils seraient	ils auraient été

Subjunctive Mood

Present.	Imperfect.	Present.	Imperfect.
j'aie	j'eusse	je sois	je fusse
tu aies	tu eusses	tu sois	tu fusses
il ait	il eût	il soit	il fût
nous ayons	nous eussions	nous soyons	nous fussions
vous ayez	vous eussiez	vous soyez	vous fussiez
ils aient	ils eussent	ils soient	ils fussent

Perfect.	Pluperfect.	Perfect.	Pluperfect.
j'aie eu	j'eusse eu	j'aie été	j'eusse été
tu aies eu	tu eusses eu	tu aies été	tu eusses été
il ait eu	il eût eu	il ait été	il eût été
nous ayons eu	nous eussions eu	nous ayons été	nous eussions été
vous ayez eu	vous eussiez eu	vous ayez été	vous eussiez été
ils aient eu	ils eussent eu	ils aient été	ils eussent été

Imperative

aie! have! (thou)	sois! be! (thou)
ayons! let us have!	soyons! let us be!
ayez! have! (you)	soyez! be! (you)

Infinitive

Present: **avoir**, to have   **être**, to be
Perfect: **avoir eu**, to have had   **avoir été**, to have been.

Participles

Present: **ayant**, having   **étant**, being
Past: **eu**, had   **été**, been
    ayant eu, having had   **ayant été**, having been

Verbs Conjugated with ÊTRE

Some verbs form their compound tenses, not with **avoir**, but with the help of the verb **être**. Here is a list of these verbs:

aller, to go	**venir**, to come; **devenir**, to become; **revenir**, to come back
arriver, to arrive	**partir**, to set out; **repartir**, to set out again
entrer, to enter	**sortir**, to go out; **ressortir**, to go out again
rentrer, to come home	**retourner**, to go back
naître, to be born	**mourir**, to die
monter, to go up	**descendre**, to go down
remonter, to go up again	**redescendre**, to go down again
tomber, to fall	**rester**, to remain
retomber, to fall again	

You will notice that most of these verbs concern motion, but do not be led into thinking that **être** is used with all verbs of motion. That is not true: **courir**, to run; **sauter**, to jump; **danser**, to dance; **marcher**, to walk, are all used with **avoir**: **j'ai couru, il avait sauté, nous avons dansé, ils auront marché.**

Compound Tenses of a Verb Conjugated with ÊTRE

Arriver, to arrive

Perfect.	Pluperfect.
I have arrived	*I had arrived*
je suis arrivé(e)	j'étais arrivé(e)
tu es arrivé(e)	tu étais arrivé(e)
il est arrivé	il était arrivé
elle est arrivée	elle était arrivée
nous sommes arrivé(e)s	nous étions arrivé(e)s
vous êtes arrivé(e)(s)	vous étiez arrivé(e)(s)
ils sont arrivés	ils étaient arrivés
elles sont arrivées	elles étaient arrivées

Past Anterior.	Future Perfect.
I had arrived	*I shall have arrived*
je fus arrivé(e)	je serai arrivé(e)
tu fus arrivé(e)	tu seras arrivé(e)
il fut arrivé	il sera arrivé
nous fûmes arrivé(e)s	nous serons arrivé(e)s
vous fûtes arrivé(e)(s)	vous serez arrivé(e)(s)
ils furent arrivés	ils seront arrivés

Conditional Perfect.

I should have arrived

je serais arrivé(e)	nous serions arrivé(e)s
tu serais arrivé(e)	vous seriez arrivé(e)(s
il serait arrivé	ils seraient arrivés

Subjunctive.

Perfect.	Pluperfect.
je sois arrivé(e)	je fusse arrivé(e)
tu sois arrivé(e)	tu fusses arrivé(e)
il soit arrivé	il fût arrivé
nous soyons arrivé(e)s	nous fussions arrivé(e)s
vous soyez arrivé(e)(s)	vous fussiez arrivé(e)(s)
ils soient arrivés	ils fussent arrivés

Infinitive.

Present: arriver, to arrive
Perfect: être arrivé(e)(s), to have arrived

Participles.

arrivé(e)(s), arrived
étant arrivé(e)(s), having arrived

Note that with this type of verb, the Past Participle agrees with the subject of the verb, the doer of the action:

> *Nous* sommes *montés* dans le train. We got into the train.
>
> *Il* était *tombé* dans l'escalier. He had fallen on the stairs.
>
> *Elle* est *née* en France et est *morte* en Italie. She was born in France and died in Italy.
>
> Mes deux *sœurs* sont *parties* pour l'Amérique. Both my sisters have left for America.

Some of the above verbs may also be conjugated with **avoir**, but they then have different meanings and can take an object.

Compare the following sentences in which **descendre**, **monter** and **rentrer** are used with **être** and **avoir**.

With être.	With avoir.
Elle est descendue du train.	Elle a descendu les bagages.
She got down from the train.	She brought the luggage downstairs.
Elle était montée à sa chambre.	Elle avait monté ma valise.
She had gone up to her room.	She had taken my case upstairs.
Elle est rentrée à six heures.	Elle a rentré mon vélo.
She came home at six.	She has brought my bicycle indoors.

THE PASSIVE VOICE

The passive voice is formed by adding the Past Participle of the verb to the correct tense of être. This is exactly the same as the English usage. Thus the Present Tense of the Passive of **punir**, to punish, goes like this:

je suis puni(e), I am punished	nous sommes puni(e)s, we are punished
tu es puni(e), thou art punished	vous êtes puni(e)(s), you are punished
il est puni, he is punished	ils sont punis, they are punished
elle est punie, she is punished	elles sont punies, they are punished

Similarly other tenses can be formed:

Past Historic: je fus puni(e), I was punished
Future: je serai puni(e), I shall be punished
Perfect: j'ai été puni(e), I have been punished
Pluperfect: j'avais été puni(e), I had been punished
Past Anterior: j'eus été puni(e), I had been punished
Future Perfect: j'aurai été puni(e), I shall have been punished
Conditional: je serais puni(e), I should be punished
Conditional Perfect: j'aurais été puni(e), I should have been punished
Present Subjunctive: je sois puni(e)
Imperfect Subjunctive: je fusse puni(e)
Perfect Subjunctive: j'aie été puni(e)
Pluperfect Subjunctive: j'eusse été puni(e)
Imperative: sois puni(e), soyons puni(e)s, soyez puni(e)(s)
Infinitive: Present: être puni(e)(s), to be punished
          Past: avoir été puni(e)(s), to have been punished
Participle: étant puni(e)(s), being punished

Note that in the Passive Voice the Past Participle agrees with the Subject of the sentence:

La jeune *fille* a été *punie.* The girl has been punished.
Les *vaches* avaient été *vendues* au marché. The cows had been sold at the market.

Avoiding the Passive

The French often avoid using the Passive Voice. Instead of a rather cumbrous sentence like

La fenêtre a été réparée. The window has been repaired.

they often prefer to say:

On a réparé la fenêtre. One has repaired the window.

Here are some other examples of how to evade the complicated Passive Voice:

It is said that . . . **On dit que** (one says that) . . .

He will be respected. **On le respectera** (one will respect him).

He was seen entering the house. **On l'a vu entrer dans la maison.**

The Passive Must not Be Used with Verbs that Take the Dative

The construction with **on** *must* be used if the French verb takes a dative (or indirect object). For instance, in French one says **répondre à une question**, to answer *to* a question; **demander à un homme**, to ask (*to*) a man; **dire à quelqu'un**, to tell *to* someone. In cases like this, the passive may not be used: one must not say in French: "his question is answered", "the man was asked", "the woman will be told". The sentences must be recast, using one (**on**).

One answers (to) his question. **On répond à sa question.**
One asked (to) the man. **On demanda à l'homme.**
One will tell (to) the woman. **On dira à la femme.**

REFLEXIVE VERBS

Reflexive Verbs are easily recognised in a dictionary: they have the word SE in front of them: **se laver**, to wash oneself; **se raser**, to shave oneself; **s'habiller**, to dress oneself. With this kind of verb, the action, instead of passing on to another person, reflects back on the doer. The subject and object are the same person; one is doing something to oneself.

Below is a simple example of a reflexive verb. Notice that in the Compound Tenses ÊTRE is used. The endings are the normal ones.

SE LAVER, to wash oneself

Indicative Mood

Present.

je me lave, I wash myself
tu te laves, thou washest thyself
il se lave, he washes himself
elle se lave, she washes herself
nous nous lavons, we wash ourselves

vous vous lavez, you wash { yourself
{ yourselves

ils se lavent }
elles se lavent } they wash themselves

Imperfect.

I was washing myself
I used to wash myself
je me lavais
tu te lavais
il se lavait
nous nous lavions
vous vous laviez
ils se lavaient

Past Historic.

I washed myself

je me lavai
tu te lavas
il se lava
nous nous lavâmes
vous vous lavâtes
ils se lavèrent

Future.

I shall wash myself

je me laverai
tu te laveras
il se lavera
nous nous laverons
vous vous laverez
ils se laveront

Compound Tenses

Perfect.

I have washed myself

je me suis lavé(e)
tu t'es lavé(e)
il s'est lavé
elle s'est lavée
nous nous sommes lavé(e)s
vous vous êtes lavé(e)(s)
ils se sont lavés
elles se sont lavées

Pluperfect.

I had washed myself

je m'étais lavé(e)
tu t'étais lavé(e)
il s'était lavé
nous nous étions lavé(e)s
vous vous étiez lavé(e)(s)
ils s'étaient lavés

Past Anterior.

I had washed myself

je me fus lavé(e)
tu te fus lavé(e)
il se fut lavé
nous nous fûmes lavé(e)s
vous vous fûtes lavé(e)(s)
ils se furent lavés

Future Perfect.

I shall have washed myself

je me serai lavé(e)
tu te seras lavé(e)
il se sera lavé
nous nous serons lavé(e)s
vous vous serez lavé(e)(s)
ils se seront lavés

Conditional Mood

Conditional.	Conditional Perfect.
I should wash myself	*I should have washed myself*
je me laverais	je me serais lavé(e)
tu te laverais	tu te serais lavé(e)
il se laverait	il se serait lavé
nous nous laverions	nous nous serions lavé(e)s
vous vous laveriez	vous vous seriez lavé(e)(s)
ils se laveraient	ils se seraient lavés

Subjunctive Mood

Present.	Imperfect.	Perfect.	Pluperfect.
je me lave	je me lavasse	je me sois lavé(e)	je me fusse lavé(e)
tu te laves	tu te lavasses	tu te sois lavé(e)	tu te fusses lavé(e)
il se lave	il se lavât	il se soit lavé	il se fût lavé
nous nous lavions	nous nous lavassions	nous nous soyons lavé(e)s	nous nous fussions lavé(e)s
vous vous laviez	vous vous lavassiez	vous vous soyez lavé(e)(s)	vous vous fussiez lavé(e)(s)
ils se lavent	ils se lavassent	ils se soient lavés	ils se fussent lavés

Imperative

lave-toi! wash thyself!
ne te lave pas! do not wash thyself
lavons-nous! let us wash ourselves!
ne nous lavons pas! let us not wash ourselves!
lavez-vous! wash { yourself! / yourselves! }

ne vous lavez pas! do not wash { yourself! / yourselves! }

Infinitive

se laver, to wash oneself   s'être lavé, to have washed oneself

Participles

se lavant, washing oneself   s'étant lavé, having washed oneself

Notice that the Reflexive Verb has the normal endings, but the Past Participle in the Compound Tenses agrees with the preceding direct object, in this case the reflexive pronouns me, te, se, nous, vous, se. This is the usual state of affairs, the reflexive pronoun being also the direct object:

Elle *s'*est *lavée*. She has washed herself.
Nous *nous* sommes *coupés*. We have cut ourselves.

However, occasionally the reflexive pronoun may be an indirect object, and then there is no agreement:

Ils se sont dit. They said to themselves.
Nous nous sommes demandé. We asked (to) ourselves.

AUXILIARY VERBS: AVOIR OR ÊTRE?

Whether to use **avoir** or être with a verb is a problem which worries every student of the French language: it even worries some Frenchmen! Let us sum up briefly.

1. *All* transitive verbs (i.e., verbs that take a direct object) and most instransitive verbs use **avoir** in compound tenses.

Il avait fait la connaissance de cette femme. He had made the acquaintance of this woman.
J'ai décidé de ne pas le faire. I decided not to do it.

2. A verb in the passive voice takes être.

J'avais vingt ans. J'aimais, j'étais aimé. I was twenty. I was in love, I was loved.
Dans ce combat Orso fut vaincu. In this fight Orso was beaten.

3. *All* reflexive verbs take être.

Elle s'est couchée tout de suite. She went to bed at once.
Je m'étais levé de bonne heure. I had got up early.

4. The following intransitive verbs: aller, arriver, entrer, rentrer, naître, monter, remonter, tomber, retomber, venir,

devenir, revenir, partir, sortir, mourir, descendre, redescendre, rester take être.

> Il est né en France. He was born in France.
> Nous y serions restés longtemps. We should have stayed there a long time.

IRREGULAR VERBS

If a verb does not behave as an -ER, -IR or -RE verb generally does, it is called an irregular verb. It simply does not obey the usual rules. Learning these verbs is one of the curses of studying a language. However, the important ones are soon learned, because, oddly enough, they include some of the most common verbs. You meet them so often that you acquire them almost unconsciously. Later on in this chapter we shall give a fairly complete list. We do not give all the tenses, because some you can easily form for yourself.

Rules for the Formation of the Tenses

1. If you know the Past Participle you can form the Compound Tenses with the help of the auxiliary **avoir** or **être**.

2. The Imperfect and Conditional of *all* verbs have the same endings: -AIS, -AIS, -AIT, -IONS, -IEZ, -AIENT.

3. The *stem* of the Future and Conditional is *always* the same: the future of **être** is **je serai**, the conditional is **je serais**; the future of **aller** is **j'irai**, the conditional is **j'irais**.

4. The Future is nearly always formed by adding endings to the Infinitive. The endings of the Future are the same for *all* verbs: -AI, -AS, -A, -ONS, -EZ, -ONT: The Future of the irregular verb **FUIR** is **je fuirai**.

5. To form the Imperfect Indicative, remove the -ONS from the 1st Person Plural of the Present Indicative of **a**

verb and add the endings -AIS, -AIS, -AIT, -IONS, -IEZ, -AIENT. Thus savoir, Present Indicative nous savons, remove the -ONS, sav-, Imperfect je savais, etc.

(The only exception to this rule is être, which has j'étais as its Imperfect.)

6. The Imperative (with the exceptions of avoir, être, savoir and vouloir) is formed from the Present Indicative by removing the pronouns from the 2nd Person Singular, 1st Person Plural and 2nd Person Plural. Thus finis, finissons, finissez. -ER verbs lose the s in the 2nd Person Singular, thus donner: donne, donnons, donnez.

7. In the Past Historic:

(a) -ER verbs have the endings -AI, -AS, -A, ÂMES, -ÂTES, -ÈRENT.

(b) Most -IR and -RE verbs end in -IS, -IS, -IT, -ÎMES, -ÎTES, -IRENT.

(c) Most verbs in -OIR and -OIRE end in -US, -US, -UT, -ÛMES, -ÛTES, -URENT.

(d) TENIR and VENIR are quite distinctive: tenir becomes tins, tins, tint, tînmes, tîntes, tinrent; venir becomes vins, vins, vint, vînmes, etc.

8. The endings of the Present Subjunctive (with the exceptions of avoir and être) are -E, -ES, -E, -IONS, -IEZ, -ENT. The stem can generally be found by removing the -ENT of the 3rd Person Plural of the Present Indicative. Thus boire, ils boivent, boiv-, je boive, etc.

If the stem of the Present Indicative changes during the tense, the stem of the Present Subjunctive generally follows suit. Thus boire, Present Indicative: bois, bois, boit, *buvons*, *buvez*, boivent; Present Subjunctive: boive, boives, boive, *buvions*, *buviez*, boivent.

9. The Imperfect Subjunctive is *always* formed by adding -SE to the 2nd Person Singular of the Past Historic. Thus venir, tu vins, je vinsse, etc.

Principal

Infinitive.	Participles.	Present Indicative.	Imperfect Past Historic.
acquérir, *to acquire*	acquérant	acquiers, -iers, -iert	acquérais
	acquis	acquérons, -érez, acquièrent	acquis
*aller, *to go*	allant	vais, vas, va	allais
	allé	allons, allez, vont	allai
asseoir, *to seat*	asseyant	assieds, assieds, assied,	asseyais
	assis	asseyons, -ez, -ent	assis
avoir, *to have*	ayant	ai, as, a,	avais
	eu	avons, avez, ont	eus
battre, *to beat*	battant	bats, bats, bat,	battais
	battu	battons, -ez, -ent	battis
boire, *to drink*	buvant	bois, bois, boit,	buvais
	bu	buvons, buvez, boivent	bus
bouillir, *to boil*	bouillant	bous, -s, -t,	bouillais
	bouilli	bouillons, -ez, -ent	bouillis
conclure, *to conclude*	concluant	conclus, -s, -t, -ent	concluais
	conclu	concluons, -ez, -ent	conclus
connaître, *to know*	connaissant	connais, -s, connaît,	connaissais
	connu	connaissons, -ez, -ent	connus
coudre, *to sew*	cousant	couds, couds, coud,	cousais
	cousu	cousons, -ez, -ent	cousis
courir, *to run*	courant	cours, -s, -t,	courais
	couru	courons, -ez, -ent	courus
couvrir, *to cover*	couvrant	couvre, -es, -e,	couvrais
	couvert	couvrons, -ez, -ent	couvris
craindre, *to fear*	craignant	crains, -s, -t,	craignais
	craint	craignons, -ez, -ent	craignis
croire, *to believe*	croyant	crois, -s, -t,	croyais
	cru	croyons, -ez, croient	crus
croître, *to grow*	croissant	croîs, croîs, croît,	croissais
	crû, crue	croissons, -ez, -ent	crûs
cueillir, *to gather*	cueillant	cueille, -es, -e,	cueillais
	cueilli	-ons, -ez, -ent	cueillis
cuire, *to cook*	cuisant	cuis, cuis, cuit,	cuisais
	cuit	cuisons, -ez, -ent	cuisis
devoir, *to owe*	devant	dois, dois, doit,	devais
to have to	dû, due	devons, devez, doivent	dus
dire, *to say*	disant	dis, -s, -t,	disais
	dit	disons, dîtes, disent	dis
dormir, *to sleep*	dormant	dors, dors, dort,	dormais
	dormi	dormons, -ez, -ent	dormis
écrire, *to write*	écrivant	écris, -s, -t,	écrivais
	écrit	écrivons, -ez, -ent	écrivis
envoyer, *to send*	envoyant	envoie, -es, -e,	envoyais
	envoyé	envoyons, -ez, envoient	envoyai
être, *to be*	étant	suis, es, est,	étais
	été	sommes, êtes, sont	fus
faillir, *to fail*	—	faut (rare)	—
	failli		faillis
faire, *to make, do*	faisant	fais, fais, fait,	faisais
	fait	faisons, faites, font	fis
falloir, *to be necessary*	—	il faut	il fallait
	fallu		il fallut
fuir, *to flee from*	fuyant	fuis, fuis, fuit,	fuyais
	fui	fuyons, -ez, fuient	fuis
haïr, *to hate*	haïssant	hais, hais, hait,	haïssais
	haï	haïssons, -ez, -ent	
joindre, *to join*	joignant	joins, -s, -t,	joignais
	joint	joignons, -ez, -ent	joignis

* Conjugated with the verb être.

Irregular Verbs

Present Subjunctive.	Future Conditional.	Imperative.	Remarks. So conjugate.
acquière, -es, -e,	acquerrai	acquiers,	conquérir
acquérions, -iez, acquièrent	acquerrais	acquérons, acquérez	
aille, ailles, aille,	irai	va,	
allions, alliez, aillent	irais	allons, allez	
asseye, -es, -e	assiérai	assieds, asseyons,	*s'asseoir
asseyions, -iez, -ent	assiérais	asseyez	
aie, aies, ait,	aurai	aie,	
ayons, ayez, aient	aurais	ayons, ayez	
batte, -es, -e,	battrai	bats, battons,	combattre
-ions, -iez, -ent	battrais	battez	abattre
boive, -es, -e,	boirai	bois, buvons,	
buvions, -iez, boivent	boirais	buvez	
bouille, -es, -e,	bouillirai	bous, bouillons,	intransitive verb, l'eau
-ions, -iez, -ent	bouillirais	bouillez	bout, *the water boils*, but je fais bouillir l'eau, *I boil the water*
conclue, -es, -e,	conclurai	conclus, concluons,	
-ions, -iez, -ent	conclurais	concluez	
connaisse, -es, -e,	connaîtrai	connais, connaissons,	paraître
-ions, -iez, -ent	connaîtrais	connaissez	
couse, -es, -e,	coudrai	couds, cousons,	
-ions, -iez, -ent	coudrais	cousez	
coure, -es, -e,	courrai	cours, courons,	
-ions, -iez, -ent	courrais	courez	
couvre, -es, -e,	couvrirai	couvre, couvrons,	ouvrir, offrir
-ions, -iez, -ent	couvrirais	couvrez	souffrir
craigne, -es, -e,	craindrai	crains, craignons,	plaindre, joindre,
-ions, -iez, -ent	craindrais	craignez	teindre, peindre
croie, -es, -e,	croirai	crois, croyons,	
croyions, -iez, croient	croirais	croyez	
croisse, -es, -e,	croîtrai	croîs, croissons,	Notice the circumflex accent to distinguish it from croire
-ions, -iez, -ent	croîtrais	croissez	
cueille, -es, -e,	cueillerai	cueille, cueillons,	accueillir
-ions, -iez, -ent	cueillerais	cueillez	
cuise, -es, -e,	cuirai	cuis, cuisons,	
-ions, -iez, -ent	cuirais	cuisez	
doive, -es, -e,	devrai	dois, devons,	Je dois cent francs, *I owe 100 francs*
devions, -iez, doivent	devrais	devez	Je dois partir, *I must go*
dise, -es, -e,	dirai	dis, disons	
-ions, -iez, -ent	dirais	dites	
dorme, -es, -e,	dormirai	dors, dormons,	mentir, *partir, servir,
-ions, -iez, -ent	dormirais	dormez	sentir, *sortir
écrive, -es, -e,	écrirai	écris, écrivons,	décrire
-ions, -iez, -ent	écrirais	écrivez	
envoie, -es, -e,	enverrai	envoie, envoyons,	
envoyions, -iez, envoient	enverrais	envoyez	
sois, sois, soit,	serai	sois, soyons,	
soyons, -ez, soient	serais	soyez	
—	faudrai	—	J'ai failli attendre, *I nearly waited*
	faudrais		
fasse, -es, -e,	ferai	fais, faisons,	
fassions, -iez, -ent	ferais	faites	
il faille	il faudra		
	il faudrait		
fuie, -es, -e,	fuirai	fuis, fuyons,	
fuyions, -iez, fuient	fuirais	fuyez	
haïsse, -es, -e,	haïrai	hais, haïssons,	
-ions, -iez, -ent	haïrais	haïssez	
joigne, -es, -e,	joindrai	joins, joignons,	plaindre, craindre,
-ions, -iez, -ent	joindrais	joignez	teindre

Principal

Infinitive.	Participles.	Present Indicative.	Imperfect Past Historic.
lire, *to read*	lisant lu	lis, lis, lit, lisons, -ez, -ent	lisais lus
luire, *to shine*	luisant lui	luis, luis, luit, luisons, -ez, -ent	luisais luisis
mentir, *to lie*	mentant menti	mens, -s, -t, mentons, -ez, -ent	mentais mentis
mettre, *to put*	mettant mis	mets, mets, met, mettons, -ez, -ent	mettais mis
moudre, *to grind*	moulant moulu	mouds, mouds, moud, moulons, -ez, -ent	moulais moulus
*mourir, *to die*	mourant mort	meurs, -s, -t, mourons, -ez, meurent	mourais mourus
mouvoir, *to move*	mouvant mû	meus, -s, -t, mouvons, -ez, meuvent	mouvais mus
*naître, *to be born*	naissant né	nais, nais, naît, naissons, -ez, -ent	naissais naquis
plaire, *to please*	plaisant plu	plais, -s, plaît, plaisons, -ez, -ent	plaisais plus
pleuvoir, *to rain*	pleuvant plu	il pleut	il pleuvait il plut
pouvoir, *to be able*	pouvant pu	puis } peux } , peux, peut, pouvons, -ez, peuvent	pouvais pus
prendre, *to take*	prenant pris	prends, prends, prend, prenons, -ez, prennent	prenais pris
recevoir, *to receive*	recevant reçu	reçois, -s, -t, recevons, -ez, reçoivent	recevais reçus
rire, *to laugh*	riant ri	ris, ris, rit, rions, riez, rient	riais ris
rompre, *to break*	rompant rompu	romps, romps, rompt, rompons, -ez, -ent	rompais rompis
savoir, *to know*	sachant su	sais, sais, sait, savons, -ez, -ent	savais sus
suffire, *to suffice*	suffisant suffi	suffis, -is, -it, suffisons, -ez, -ent	suffisais suffis
suivre, *to follow*	suivant suivi	suis, suis, suit, suivons, -ez, -ent	suivais suivis
taire, *to silence*	taisant tu	tais, tais, taît, taisons, taisez, taisent	taisais tus
tenir, *to hold*	tenant tenu	tiens, tiens, tient, tenons, tenez, tiennent	tenais tins
tressaillir, *to quiver*	tressaillant tressailli	tressaille, -es, -e, -ons, -ez, -ent	tressaillais tressaillis
vaincre, *to conquer*	vainquant vaincu	vaincs, vaincs, vainc, vainquons, vainquez, vainquent	vainquais vainquis
valoir, *to be worth*	valant valu	vaux, vaux, vaut, valons, valez, valent	valais valus
*venir, *to come*	venant venu	viens, viens, vient, venons, venez, viennent	venais vins
vêtir, *to dress*	vêtant vêtu	vêts, vêts, vêt, vêtons, vêtez, vêtent	vêtais vêtis
vivre, *to live*	vivant vécu	vis, vis, vit, vivons, -ez, -ent	vivais vécus
voir, *to see*	voyant vu	vois, -s, -t, voyons, -ez, voient	voyais vis
vouloir, *to wish*	voulant voulu	veux, veux, veut, voulons, voulez, veulent	voulais voulus

* Conjugated with the verb être.

Irregular Verbs

Present Subjunctive.	Future Conditional.	Imperative.	Remarks. So conjugate.
lise, -es, -e,	lirai	lis, lisons,	élire
-ions, -iez, -ent	lirais	lisez	
luise, -es, -e,	luirai	luis, luisons,	
-ions, -iez, -ent	luirais	luisez	
mente, -es, -e,	mentirai	mens, mentons,	*sortir, *partir
-ions, -iez, -ent	mentirais	mentez	
mette, -es, -e,	mettrai	mets, mettons,	
-ions, -iez, -ent	mettrais	mettez	
moule, -es, -e,	moudrai	mouds, moulons,	
-ions, -iez, -ent	moudrais	moulez	
meure, -es, -e,	mourrai	meurs, mourons,	
mourions, -iez, meurent	mourrais	mourez	
meuve, -es, -e,	mouvrai	meus, mouvons,	
mouvions, -iez, meuvent	mouvrais	mouvez	
naisse, -es, -e,	naîtrai	nais, naissons,	
-ions, -iez, -ent	naîtrais	naissez	
plaise, -es, -e,	plairai	plais, plaisons,	déplaire
-ions, -iez, ent	plairais	plaisez	
il pleuve	il pleuvra	qu'il pleuve	
	il pleuvrait		
puisse, -es, -e,	pourrai	—	
-ions, -iez, -ent	pourrais		
prenne, -es, -e,	prendrai	prends, prenons,	comprendre
prenions, -iez, prennent	prendrais	prenez	
reçoive, -es, -e,	recevrai	reçois, recevons,	
recevions, -iez, reçoivent	recevrais	recevez	
rie, ries, rie,	rirai	ris, rions,	sourire
riions, -iez, -ent	rirais	riez	
rompe, -es, -e,	romprai	romps, rompons	corrompre,
-ions, -iez, -ent	romprais	rompez	interrompre
sache, -es, -e,	saurai	sache, sachons,	
-ions, -iez, -ent	saurais	sachez	
suffise, -es, -e,	suffirai	suffis, suffisons,	
-ions, -iez, -ent	suffirais	suffisez	
suive, -es, -e,	suivrai	suis, suivons,	poursuivre
-ions, -iez, -ent	suivrais	suivez	
taise, -es, -e,	tairai	tais, taisons,	
-ions, -iez, -ent	tairais	taisez	
tienne, -es, -e,	tiendrai	tiens, tenons,	
tenions, -iez, tiennent	tiendrais	tenez	
tressaille, -es, -e,	tressaillirai	tressaille, tressaillons,	
-ions, iez, -ent	tressaillirais	tressaillez	
vainque, -es, -e,	vaincrai	vaincs, vainquons,	
-ions, iez, -ent	vaincrais	vainquez	
vaille, -es, -e,	vaudrai	—	
valions, -iez, vaillent	vaudrais		
vienne, -es, -e,	viendrai	viens, venons,	*devenir
venions, -iez, viennent	viendrais	venez	*revenir
vête, -es, -e,	vêtirai	vêts, vêtons,	
-ions, -iez, -ent	vêtirais	vêtez	
vive, -es, -e,	vivrai	vis, vivons,	
-ions, -iez, -ent	vivrais	vivez	
voie, -es, -e,	verrai	vois, voyons,	entrevoir
voyions, voyiez, voient	verrais	voyez	prévoir (fut. prévoirai)
veuille, -es, -e,	voudrai	veuille, veuillons,	
voulions, vouliez, veuillent	voudrais	veuillez	

You will notice that not even irregular verbs are different all the time. They are irregular only in certain tenses.

IMPERSONAL VERBS

Impersonal Verbs are verbs used in the 3rd Person Singular only. Examples are neiger, to snow: il neige, it snows; il neigeait, it was snowing; pleuvoir, to rain: il pleut, it is raining; il a plu, it has been raining; il pleuvra, it will rain. Two very important ones which require more explanation are FALLOIR (to be necessary) and IL Y A * (there is, there are). Here are their tenses and meanings:

Y AVOIR	FALLOIR
Present: il y a, there is, there are	il faut, it is necessary
Imperfect:	il fallait, it was (used to be) necessary
il y avait, {there was, were / there used to be}	
Past Historic: il y eut, there was, were	il fallut, it was necessary
Future: il y aura, there will be	il faudra, it will be necessary
Perfect: il y a eu, there has (have) been	il a fallu, it has been necessary
Pluperfect: il y avait eu, there had been	il avait fallu, it had been necessary
Past Anterior: il y eut eu, there had been	il eut fallu, it had been necessary
Future Perfect: il y aura eu, there will have been	il aura fallu, it will have been necessary
Conditional: il y aurait, there would be	il faudrait, it would be necessary
Conditional Perfect: il y aurait eu, there would have been	il aurait fallu, it would have been necessary
Present Subjunctive: il y ait	il faille
Imperfect Subjunctive: il y eût	il fallût
Perfect Subjunctive: il y ait eu	il ait fallu
Pluperfect Subjunctive: il y eût eu	il eût fallu

* Do not confuse il y a with voilà (also meaning "there is" or "there are"), which may be used in conversation only when you are actually pointing to someone or something.

Examples

1. Y AVOIR.

Il y a beaucoup de monde dans les rues. There are a lot of people in the streets.

Il y aura deux cents personnes au bal. There will be two hundred people at the dance.

Il y a is also used with the sense of "ago".

il y a une semaine, a week ago

il y a dix jours, ten days ago

2. FALLOIR.

Il faut aller à l'hôpital.
{ It is necessary to go to the hospital.
You must go to the hospital.
One must go to the hospital.

Il me faudra lire le livre.
{ It will be necessary for me to read the book.
I shall have to read the book.

Il faut de la patience.
{ It is necessary (to have) patience.
Patience is needed.

HOW TO MAKE A VERB NEGATIVE

The French equivalent for "not" with a verb is made up of two words, **ne** and **pas**. Ne (n' before a vowel or mute h) is placed before the verb, pas almost always comes after.

J'aime, I like Je n'aime pas, I do not like

il parlait, he was speaking il ne parlait pas, he was not speaking

In compound tenses, **ne** or **n'** comes before the auxiliary verb **avoir** or **être**, pas is placed before the Past Participle.

il était entré, he had entered il n'était pas entré, he had not entered

nous aurions cru, we should have thought nous n'aurions pas cru, we should not have thought

In the case of the Infinitive, both **ne** and **pas** are put before the verb:

> **Je préfère ne pas y aller ce soir.** I prefer not to go there tonight.

THE INTERROGATIVE

To turn a verb into its question form, the pronoun is placed after the verb or, in the compound tenses, after its auxiliary. Thus:

> **Vous venez.** You come.
> **Venez-vous?** Are you coming?
> **Ils ne voient pas.** They do not see.
> **Ne voient-ils pas?** Do they not see?
> **J'ai fini.** I have finished.
> **Ai-je fini?** Have I finished?
> **Vous n'êtes pas sorti.** You did not go out.
> **N'êtes-vous pas sorti?** Did you not go out?

In the 3rd Person Singular of the Present Tense of the -ER conjugation, in the 3rd Person Singular of the Future Tense of all verbs, in the 3rd Person Singular of the Past Historic of -ER verbs and of the Present Tense of **avoir**, the letter **t** is inserted before the **il** or the **elle** in order to prevent a clash of vowels:

il donne, he gives | donne-t-il? does he give?
elle fera, she will make | fera-t-elle? will she make?
il envoya, he sent | envoya-t-il? did he send?
elle a, she has | a-t-elle? has she?

When the subject of the verb is a noun the noun is placed first, followed by the verb and the corresponding pronoun:

> **Mes parents sont ici.** My parents are here.
> **Mes parents sont-ils ici?** Are my parents here?
> **L'autobus n'est pas parti.** The bus has not left.
> **L'autobus n'est-il pas parti?** Has not the bus left?

An alternative method of making a verb interrogative is to put **Est-ce que** (is it that?) before the verb without altering the word order. As this way avoids the use of inversion, it is very frequently used in conversation.

> **Il va.** He goes.
> **Est-ce qu'il va?** Is he going?
> **Vous parlez.** You speak.
> **Est-ce que vous parlez?** Are you speaking?
> **Les parents sont déjà partis.** The parents have already left.
> **Est-ce que les parents sont déjà partis?** Have the parents already left?
> **Où est-ce que vous avez vu mon père?** Where did you see my father?

This **Est-ce que** method is also the usual one for the 1st Person Singular of the Present Tense of **-ER** verbs. One always says and writes **Est-ce que je donne?** Am I giving? and one uses est-ce que with most monosyllabic forms: **est-ce que je crains?** do I fear? where the alternatives would give a harsh sound. On the other hand, the forms **ai-je?** have I?; **dois-je?** must I?; **puis-je?** may I?; **sais-je?** do I know?; **vais-je?** am I going?; **suis-je?** am I? are very common.

A further method of forming the Interrogative is to make a statement and follow it by **n'est-ce pas?** (is it not?).

> **Il est intelligent, n'est-ce pas?** He is intelligent, isn't he?
> **Nous allons à Paris, n'est-ce pas?** We are going to Paris, aren't we?
> **Elles sont déjà arrivées, n'est-ce pas?** They have already arrived, haven't they?

Note that whatever person or tense is used, **n'est-ce pas** remains unchanged.

USING THE TENSES AND MOODS

In this section we shall mention only those tenses which are likely to prove difficult to the student.

The Infinitive

The infinitive may be used as subject, complement or object of a verb and also after a preposition.

> **Voir c'est croire,** to see is to believe
> **je veux chanter,** I want to sing
> **il aime à rire,** he loves to laugh
> **sans mentir,** without telling lies
> **pour réussir,** in order to succeed
> **afin de s'amuser,** in order to enjoy oneself

It is also occasionally used on public notices as an imperative:

> **Ne pas se pencher au dehors!** Do not lean out!

in a few expressions like:

> **Que faire?** What's to be done?

and as an exclamation:

> **Mentir tout le temps! Quelle horreur!** Tell lies all the time! Ugh!

The Present Indicative

Do not forget that the Present Tense **je donne** may have three possible translations into English: I give, I am giving, I do give. The "am" and the "do" are generally used to translate the negative or interrogative forms:

> **Je ne crois pas.** I don't think.
> **Y allez-vous?** Are you going there?

As in English, the Present is also used to express an immediate future:

> **Cet après-midi je pars pour Avignon.** This afternoon I am leaving for Avignon.

There is also a dramatic use of the Present, the so-called Historic Present, where an author uses the tense to make an account of past events more vivid and exciting:

> **À ce moment, quelque chose pousse la porte, l'ouvre doucement et entre dans ma chambre.** At that moment, something pushes the door, opens it gently and comes into my bedroom.

The Present is also employed, generally in conjunction with the preposition **depuis,** to describe an action already begun but still unfinished.

> **Je suis ici depuis trois heures.** I have been here for three hours (and I'm still here!)
>
> **Il attend depuis longtemps.** He has been waiting a long time (and he's still waiting!)
>
> **J'étudie le français depuis cinq ans!**
> **Il y a cinq ans que j'étudie le français!** } I have been studying French for five years (and I'm still at it!)

The Imperfect Indicative

The usual translations of the Imperfect are "was (were)" and "used to".

1. It is used to describe an action that was going on when another took place:

> **Il descendait la rue quand il remarqua quelque chose de curieux.** He was going down the street when he noticed something strange.

2. Or an habitual action in the past:

> **Il quittait son bureau tous les jours à la même heure.** He { used to / would } leave his office every day at the same time.

3. It is also the tense of description:

Monsieur Dubois avait les yeux bleus. Mr. Dubois had blue eyes.

Le soleil brillait dans le ciel bleu, les oiseaux chantaient dans les haies. The sun shone (was shining) in the blue sky, the birds were singing (sang) in the hedges.

4. The Imperfect is used in conjunction with the preposition depuis to describe an action, already begun, which *was* still going on at the time of the narrative.

Il pleuvait depuis trois jours. It had been raining for days (and was still raining at the time!).

Il attendait l'autobus depuis vingt minutes quand j'arrivai en voiture. He had been waiting twenty minutes for the bus when I arrived in my car (when I arrived, he *was* still waiting).

The Past Historic

The Past Historic (also called the Preterite, the Past Definite or the Simple Past in some grammar-books) is the tense used in a narrative to bring the story one step forward. It describes what happened next.

Il se leva de sa chaise, courut vers la porte, l'ouvrit et descendit vite l'escalier. He got up from his chair, ran to the door, opened it and quickly went downstairs.

It is also the tense used to describe actions in the past which are considered as finished for good and all, having no connection with the present.

Louis XIV mourut en 1715 : il régna soixante-douze ans. Louis XIV died in 1715 : he reigned for seventy-two years.

Apart from a few parts of verbs used in Southern France, the Past Historic is never used in *spoken* French (unless, of course, the speaker is quoting from a book or newspaper).

It is the past tense used for events described in books, news-papers, etc. In conversation we should say, instead of the sentence above:

> Louis XIV est mort en 1715: il a régné soixante-douze ans.

The Perfect Indicative

The Perfect has the same meaning as the Past Historic, which it replaces in conversation and letter-writing. Remember that J'ai écrit may mean "I have written" or "I wrote" (or indeed "I did write" in negative or interrogative sentences).

> Elle répondit «Je ne l'ai pas fait. Je suis allée en ville ce matin et je ne suis rentrée qu'à midi et demi.» She replied: "I did not do it. I went to town this morning and didn't get back until half past twelve."

The Pluperfect Indicative and the Past Anterior

The Pluperfect Indicative and the Past Anterior have the same meaning. J'avais donné, j'eus donné, both mean "I had given". However, in a compound sentence introduced by a conjunction of time, such as après que, after; quand or lorsque (when); aussitôt que or dès que (as soon as), these conjunctions are followed by the Past Anterior if the verb in the Main Clause is in the Past Historic.*

$$\left.\begin{array}{l}\text{Après que}\\\text{Quand}\\\text{Lorsque}\\\text{Aussitôt que}\\\text{Dès que}\end{array}\right\}\text{Jean eut fini de lire son livre, il se coucha.}$$

$$\left.\begin{array}{l}\text{After}\\\text{When}\\\text{As soon as}\end{array}\right\}\text{Jean had finished reading his book, he went to bed.}$$

* Often in conversation, where the Past Historic is, of course, never used, a kind of compound tense replaces the Past Anterior: Quand Jean a eu fini de lire son livre, il s'est couché.

There is a similar construction, but with inversion after—

> à peine . . . que, hardly (scarcely) . . . than
> À peine le voleur fut-il entré dans la maison que l'agent sauta sur lui. Scarcely had the robber entered the house than the policeman jumped on him.

If there is no conjunction of time, the Pluperfect is used.

> À vingt ans, j'avais fini mes études. At the age of twenty I had finished my studies.
> Il en avait déjà parlé à son père. He had already spoken of it to his father.

The Future

The Future describes an action that is to come:

> Il pleuvra demain. It will rain tomorrow.
> Je partirai sans toi si tu n'es pas sage. I shall leave without you if you are not well-behaved.
> Un seul Dieu tu adoreras. One God only shalt thou worship.

In addition to translating "shall" and "will", the Future is sometimes used in French where we should use a Present in English, especially after conjunctions of time like quand, lorsque, when; aussitôt que, dès que, as soon as.

> Quand vous irez en vacances, n'oubliez pas de m'envoyer une carte. When you (will) go on holiday, don't forget to send me a card.

A similar use of the Future Perfect for the English Perfect is made:

> Aussitôt que vous aurez écrit la lettre, vous viendrez me la montrer. As soon as you (will) have written the letter, you will come and show it to me.

Do not be tempted into using the Future after the conjunction "if". "If" is never followed by the Future or Conditional.

> **S'il pleut demain, je resterai à la maison.** If it rains tomorrow, I shall stay at home.

"Shall" and "will" are not always a sign of the Future Tense. When "shall" indicates duty or obligation the verb **devoir**, to have to, should be used.

> **Vous devez obéir.** You shall obey. ($=$ You have to $\big\}$ obey.)
>   must

Willingness or determination are expressed by **vouloir**, to wish:

> **Voulez-vous entrer?** Will you come in?
> **Je ne veux pas le faire.** I will not do it.

The Conditional ("should" or "would")

The Conditional has two main uses. It is used in conjunction with the Imperfect in sentences like this:

> **S'il pleuvait, j'irais au cinéma.** If it were to rain, I should go to the cinema.

Similarly, the Conditional Perfect is used with the Pluperfect:

> **S'il avait plu, je serais allé au cinéma.** If it had rained, I should have gone to the cinema.

It is also a common tense in reported speech:

> **Il dit qu'il le ferait tout de suite.** He said that he would do it at once.

After conjunctions of time, the Conditional is used where in English we should put the Imperfect:

> **Je leur dis de partir quand ils seraient prêts.** I told them to leave when they were (would be) ready.

Similarly, the Conditional Perfect replaces the English Pluperfect:

> Il promit de venir quand il aurait fini son travail. He promised to come when he had (would have) finished his work.

The Conditional Mood is also used to make a statement when the writer is not quite ready to vouch for its authenticity.

> D'après le journal, il serait arrivé à Paris hier soir. According to the paper, he arrived in Paris last night.

Another curious use of the Conditional is to put it after Quand or Quand même to translate "though" or "even if":

> Quand même il me le dirait, je ne le croirais pas. Even if he told me so, I should not believe it.

Lastly, do not forget that "should" may, in certain circumstances, mean "ought to", in which case the verb devoir is used.

> You should (ought to) drink less wine. Vous devriez boire moins de vin.

The Imperative Mood

The Imperative has three forms only: viens! come (thou)!; venons! let us come!; venez! come (you)! If a third person is required, it is borrowed from the Present Subjunctive: qu'il entre! let him come in! qu'ils meurent! let them die!

AGREEMENT OF VERB AND SUBJECT

As a general rule, the verb agrees in number with the subject. If the subject is singular, so is the verb; a plural subject has a plural verb.

> L'homme disparut. The man disappeared.
> Les hommes disparurent. The men disappeared.

It is when we have a collective noun as subject that trouble appears. Even in English most of us do not know whether to say "The Government has decided" or "The Government have decided". In French we use a singular verb if the collective noun is in the singular:

> **Après la révolution, le clergé avait perdu toute sa richesse.** After the revolution the clergy had lost all its wealth.
>
> **L' ennemi va nous attaquer demain.** The enemy is going to attack us tomorrow.

If, however, the collective noun is followed by a plural complement, the verb may be put into the singular or plural: it depends whether the writer is thinking of an undivided whole or a number of individuals:

> **Une partie des soldats se sauva (or se sauvèrent).** A section of the soldiers ran away.

Beaucoup, many; **peu,** few; **combien,** how many; **trop,** too many; **la plupart,** most, the majority, all take a plural verb:

> **La plupart des habitants ont quitté la ville.** Most of the inhabitants have left the town.
>
> **Peu de gens croient cela.** Few people believe that.

What happens when a verb has more than one subject? With **ni . . . ni . . . ne,** neither . . . nor, the verb is generally in the plural:

> **Ni son père ni sa mère ne sont ici.** Neither his father nor his mother is here.

In the case of **l'un et l'autre** (both) and **l'un ou l'autre** (either), you are free to use a singular or plural verb:

> **L'un et l'autre arrivèrent (or arriva).** Both arrived.
>
> **L'un ou l'autre arriva (or arrivèrent).** Either arrived.

When the subjects are of different persons, great care must be exercised. Suppose the subject is **Mon frère et moi,** my brother and I, then obviously the verb must go into the 1st Person Plural: "my brother and I" can be replaced by "we":

Mon frère et moi sommes bien contents de vous revoir.
My brother and I are very pleased to see you again.

Similarly, any other combination can be solved in the same way. **Vous et votre père,** you and your father, will have a verb in the 2nd Person Plural—**vous,** you.

Vous et votre père partirez aujourd'hui. You and your father will leave today.

SOME AUXILIARY VERBS

There are a number of very important verbs which are often used before the Infinitive of other verbs: here is a list with some examples:

(*a*) **aller,** to go

Je vais l'accompagner. I am going to accompany him.

(*b*) **devoir,** to have to

Present: **Je dois parler.** I have to, I must speak.
Imperfect: **Je devais parler.** I used to have to speak, I had to speak.
Past Historic: **Je dus obéir.** I had to obey.
Future: **Je devrai me laver.** I shall have to wash myself.
Perfect: **J'ai dû le faire.** I had to do it, I must have done it.
Conditional: **Je devrais écrire.** I ought to (I should) write.
Conditional Perfect: **J'aurais dû le faire.** I ought to have done it, I should have done it.

(*c*) **pouvoir,** to be able

Present: **Je peux le porter.** I can carry it.
Puis-je entrer? May I come in?

Imperfect: **Je pouvais faire cela quand j'étais jeune.**
I was able to (I could) do that when I was young.

Conditional: **Je pourrais y aller si je voulais.** I should
be able to (could) go there if I wanted to.

Conditional Perfect: **J'aurais pu le faire si j'avais été
là.** I should have been able to do it (I could have
done it, might have done it) if I had been there.

Note that the Imperfect and the Conditional both can
mean "could".

(d) **savoir**, to know * (how to)

Present: **Je sais jouer du piano.** I can (know how to)
play the piano.

Imperfect: **Je savais bien parler le français.** I could
(used to know how to) speak French well.

You will have noticed that both **pouvoir** and **savoir** may
mean "can" or "could". **Pouvoir** is used when we refer to a
physical ability or permission, **savoir** when we mention an
ability one has learnt by a mental process. Thus:

I can speak French. **Je sais parler français.**
He cannot walk (because he has broken his leg). **Il ne
peut pas marcher.**

(e) **venir**, to come

Venez me voir demain. Come and see me tomorrow.

venir à, to happen to

Un homme vint à passer. A man happened to pass by.

venir de, to have just (found in two tenses only, the
Present and Imperfect).

Present: **il vient d'arriver**, he has just arrived
Imperfect: **il venait d'arriver**, he had just arrived.

---

* Connaître also means "to know", but in the sense of "to be
acquainted with".
Je connais son frère. I know his brother.
Connaissez-vous bien Paris? Do you know Paris well?

CONSTRUCTIONS AFTER THE VERB FAIRE, TO MAKE, TO CAUSE TO

As is the case with all French verbs, a verb dependent on another is put into the Infinitive:

Je vous fais travailler. I make you work.
Il a fait pleurer Marie. He made Mary cry.
Il fera lire l'élève. He will make the pupil read.
Il la fera lire. He will make her read.

Faire, when used in this way, can also mean "to cause":

Il fait bâtir une maison.
{ He is causing a house to be built.
He is having a house built.

If the dependent infinitive has an object of its own the object of faire becomes indirect:

Il fera lire la fillette. He will make the girl read.
Il la fera lire. He will make her read.
but Il fera lire le livre à la fillette. He will make the girl read the book.
Il lui fera lire le livre. He will make her read the book.
Il le lui fera lire. He will make her read it.

As the above sentence Il fera lire le livre à la fillette may be ambiguous, meaning either "He will make the girl read the book" or "He will cause the book to be read to the girl", it is better in cases like this to change to:

Il fera lire le livre par la fillette. He will have the book read by the girl.

When a reflexive verb is used, the reflexive pronoun is often omitted:

Je les fais asseoir. I make them sit down (s'asseoir).
Nous la faisons taire. We make her keep silence (se taire).

Similar constructions are used with the verbs voir, to see; entendre, to hear; laisser, to let, allow.

Il vous a vu venir. He saw you coming.

Je l'ai entendu parler de cela. I heard him talking about that.

Ils ne vont pas nous laisser sortir. They are not going to let us get out.

THE DEPENDENT INFINITIVE

As we mentioned above, when two verbs are used together in French, the second one is put into the Infinitive:

(a) Je l'entends jouer. I hear him playing.
(b) Il aime à chanter. He likes singing.
(c) Elle résolut de partir. She decided to set out.
(d) Vous finirez par accepter. You will end up by accepting.

The infinitive may, as you can see from the above examples, follow immediately the previous verb (a) or be separated from it by à (b), de (c) or par (d). To know whether to put in a preposition and which one to use is one of the most difficult features of French grammar. Here is a list of common French verbs together with the preposition which follows them and separates them from the next verb:

aider à	décider de	faire
aimer mieux	se dépêcher de	falloir
aller	désirer	finir de
s'amuser à	devoir	s'habituer à
apprendre à	empêcher de	se hâter de
avoir à	entendre	hésiter à
avoir peur de	entrer	inviter à
cesser de	envoyer	laisser
commencer à	espérer	se mettre à
consentir à	dire de	monter
continuer à	essayer de	ordonner de
craindre de	éviter de	oser
croire	s'excuser de	oublier de

passer son temps à	prier de	réussir à
perdre son temps à	promettre de	savoir
permettre de	proposer de	sembler
pouvoir	refuser de	se souvenir de
préférer	regretter de	tâcher de
paraître	remercier de	voir
parler de	retourner	vouloir
se préparer à		

Thus, using the above information, one says:

> Il se met à courir. He starts running.
>
> Nous hésitons à le dire. We hesitate to say so.
>
> Il m'a empêché de parler. He prevented me from speaking.
>
> Vous n'osez pas entrer. You dare not go in.

THE PRESENT PARTICIPLE

1. The Present Participle can be used as an adjective and then follows the usual rules of agreement: **votre charmante sœur**, your *charming* sister; **des soucoupes volantes**, *flying* saucers.

2. It can also assume the functions of a finite verb, having objects or being qualified by adverbs. It is then invariable.

> Cherchant un appartement, nous avons consulté tous les habitants du quartier. Looking for a flat, we consulted everybody in the district.

3. En with the Present Participle: **en chantant**, singing, while singing, by singing; as I, you, he, she, we, etc., sing, sang, etc.

> En faisant ceci, vous vous ferez détester. By doing this you will cause yourself to be hated.
>
> Il traversa la rue en courant. He ran across the street (he crossed while running).

4. **Tout en** with the *Present Participle* is used when the two actions are occurring at the same time.

> **Tout en descendant la rue, il lisait son journal.** While going down the street, he read his paper.

English Present Participle Translated by the French Infinitive

When using the Present Participle in this way with the function of a verb, remember that the Present Participle refers to the subject of the sentence. We should not use it in a sentence like this:

I saw him coming downstairs.

"I" is the subject of the sentence, while the person coming downstairs is "he". In cases like this, to avoid ambiguity we must use a dependent infinitive:

> **Je l'ai vu descendre l'escalier.**

English Present Participle Translated by a French Past Participle

Be careful when translating "sitting, kneeling, lying, hanging", etc. The French consider these to be past participles, **assis, agenouillé, couché, pendu,** because any action involved has already been accomplished.

> **Elle était assise * au coin du feu.** She was sitting (seated) at the fireside.
> **Il est agenouillé devant l'autel.** He is kneeling before the altar.
> **Le chien est couché au soleil.** The dog is lying in the sun.

Appuyé, leaning; **étendu,** lying; **accroupi,** squatting; **penché,** leaning, stooping; **accroché,** hanging from a hook, are similarly used.

---

* Be careful not to confuse **être assis,** to be sitting or seated, with **s'asseoir,** to seat oneself, to take a seat, to sit down.

Elle est assise. She is sitting.
Elle s'assied. She sits down.

English Continuous Tenses

Do not use a participle when translating English continuous tenses into French:

I am speaking. **Je parle.** (I speak.)

He was speaking. **Il parlait.**

She had been writing. **Elle avait écrit.** (She had written.)

English -ING after a Preposition

All prepositions, with the exception of EN are followed by an infinitive.

without speaking, **sans parler**

before going, **avant d'aller**

THE AGREEMENT OF THE PAST PARTICIPLE

1. The Past Participle too may be used alone as an adjective agreeing with the noun it qualifies:

une table couverte d'une nappe blanche, a table *covered* with a white cloth

des soldats blessés, *wounded* soldiers

une bouteille cassée, a *broken* bottle

2. When, however, the Past Participle is used as part of a compound tense it agrees like an adjective with its direct object, provided that this object precedes the verb. When the object follows the verb, there is no agreement:

Il *nous* a *vus.* He has seen us.

Il a *vu les hommes.* He has seen the men.

Elle *s'*est *lavée.* She washed herself.

Elle a *lavé la table.* She washed the table.

Voici les *lettres* que nous avons *écrites.* Here are the letters that we wrote.

Nous avons *écrit les lettres.* We wrote the letters.

Elle *s'*est *coupée* au doigt. She cut herself on the finger.

Elle s'est *coupé le doigt.* She cut her finger.

3. You will notice from the last two examples above that it is necessary to use special care with reflexive verbs. Where the reflexive pronoun is the direct object of the verb the past participle agrees with it:

Elle *s'est blessée.* She has hurt *herself.*
Ils *se* sont *lavés.* They have washed *themselves.*

However, the reflexive pronoun may be an indirect object: study the following examples:

Elle s'est dit. She said to herself.
Ils se sont menti. They lied to themselves.

Here there is no agreement.

A frequent case of this usage is found in the type of sentence in which the reflexive pronoun is used with a part of the body:

Elle s'est *coupé* la *main.* She has cut her hand (the hand to herself).

There is no agreement because the direct object, la main, comes after the verb.

A few reflexive verbs like se souvenir, to remember; s'apercevoir, to realise; se moquer, to mock, make fun of; se taire, to be silent, cannot take an object either direct or indirect, and their Past Participles always agree with the reflexive pronoun.

Ils se sont moqués de moi. They made fun of me.
Elle s'est souvenue de son nom. She remembered his name.
Les oiseaux se sont tus. The birds kept silent.

4. Now let us return to those verbs mentioned on page 58, which form their compound tenses with être: aller, venir, arriver, partir, entrer, sortir, naître, mourir, monter, descendre, tomber, rester, retourner. These are intransitive verbs and cannot agree with an object: they agree with the subject.

Ma *mère* est *née* à Paris. My mother was born in Paris.

Ses *sœurs* étaient *restées* à la maison. His sisters had stayed at home.

Le *père* et la *mère* n'y sont pas *retournés*. The father and mother did not go back there.

5. In the Passive Voice the Past Participle is really an adjective describing the subject and agrees with it.

Madeleine a été invitée au bal. Madeleine has been invited to the dance.

La table sera couverte d'une belle nappe. The table will be covered with a beautiful cloth.

Some Exceptions

The Past Participle does not agree with a preceding direct object which refers to price, weight or distance:

Les quelques *francs* que ce crayon m'a *coûté* . . . The few francs that this pencil cost me . . .

Les six *kilomètres* que nous avons *marché* . . . The six kilometres that we walked . . .

There is also no agreement with the pronoun EN.

Des serpents! J'*en* ai *vu* au bord de la route. Snakes! I saw some on the roadside.

THE SUBJUNCTIVE MOOD

Everyone, even French people,* finds it difficult to use the Subjunctive correctly. My advice is to find sentences which do not require this mood!

Use of the Subjunctive

(1) *Principal Clauses*

We rarely find the Subjunctive in principal clauses except in time-honoured expressions like **Vive le roi!** Long live the

---

* For instance, the Imperfect Subjunctive is practically never used in conversation. It would sound too unpleasant to a Frenchman.

King!; **Plût à Dieu que** . . . Would to God that . . . ;
Advienne que pourra! Come what may! The Present Subjunctive is sometimes used to form a 3rd Person Singular
for the Imperative: **Qu'il meure!** May he die!; **qu'ils entrent!**
let them come in!

(2) *The Subjunctive in Subordinate Clauses*

It is in subordinate clauses that the subjunctive is most
frequently used. We find it:

(*a*) After certain conjunctions. Here are the most
common—

quoique
bien que } although   **sans que,** without

pour que
afin que } in order that   **jusqu'à ce que,** until

avant que, before   **pourvu que,** provided that
à moins que . . . ne, unless

de peur que . . . ne
de crainte que . . . ne } for fear that

Quoiqu'il n'ait que vingt-trois ans, il est déjà docteur.
Although he is only twenty-three, he is already a
doctor.

Pourvu qu'il fasse beau! Provided (if only) the weather
is fine!

Nous attendrons jusqu'à ce qu'il arrive. We shall wait
until he arrives.

You will have noticed that three of these conjunctions,
à moins que, de peur que, de crainte que, have an expletive
or untranslated ne before the following verb:

à moins que vous n'y alliez tout de suite . . . unless you
go there at once . . .

de peur qu'il ne vienne . . . for fear that he may come . . .

(*b*) After verbs and expressions of emotion: to be glad,
to be sorry, to fear, etc.:

Je suis content que vous soyez ici. I am pleased that you are here.

Il regrette que je sois malade. He is sorry that I am ill.

Je ne crains pas qu'il vienne. I am not afraid* of him coming.

(c) After verbs of wishing, desiring or doubting:

Je veux que vous y alliez ce soir. I want you to go there tonight.

Maman préfère que je rentre avant dix heures. Mother prefers me to be home before ten o'clock.

(d) After verbs of thinking, believing or saying used negatively or interrogatively:

Croyez-vous qu'il soit mort? Do you think that he is dead?

Je ne dis pas que vous ayez tort. I am not saying that you are wrong.

(e) After verbs of commanding, permitting and forbidding:

Nous exigeons qu'on nous réponde. We demand that we be answered.

Je défends que vous vous absentiez ainsi. I forbid you to be absent like this.

(f) After superlatives and the words premier, first; dernier, last; seul, only; unique, only.

C'est la plus belle femme que j'aie jamais vue. She's the most beautiful woman I have ever seen.

(g) After impersonal verbs and expressions which do *not* express probability or certainty.

Il faut que vous soyez de retour avant neuf heures. It is necessary for you to be back before nine o'clock.

Il semble que j'aie tort. It seems that I am wrong.

* If a verb of fearing is used in the affirmative, an expletive ne is placed before the following verb:

Je crains qu'il ne vienne ici. I'm afraid that he will come here.

Imperfect or Present Subjunctive?

It is sometimes necessary to decide whether to use the Imperfect or Present Subjunctive. If the main verb is in the Present, Perfect, or Future of the Indicative, the Present Subjunctive is used after it; in other cases use the Imperfect Subjunctive.

> Je préfère que vous arriviez à temps. I prefer you to arrive on time.
>
> Je préférerais que vous arrivassiez à temps. I should prefer you to arrive on time.

However, even here, most Frenchmen would avoid the unpleasant-sounding Imperfect Subjunctive and say:

> Je préférerais que vous arriviez à temps.

EÛT and FÛT

You will probably come across the Imperfect Subjunctive of avoir and être, especially the forms eût and fût, used in literary French for none of the above reasons. They are considered an elegant way of expressing aurait and serait.

> S'il eût trouvé cela, il eût renvoyé tout le monde. If he had found that, he would have dismissed everyone.

The Subjunctive with QUEL QUE, QUELQUE QUE, QUI QUE, QUOI QUE

Whatever (adjective with être).

> Quels que soient vos talents, vous ne réussirez pas sans travailler. Whatever your talents may be, you will not succeed without working.

Whatever (adjective with a noun).

> Quelques talents que vous ayez, vous ne réussirez pas ... Whatever talents you may have, you will not succeed ...

However (adverb).

> Si
> Quelque } fatigués que vous soyez, marchez toujours!
> However tired you may be, keep on walking!

> Si
> Quelque } vite que nous marchions, nous ne serons pas
> là avant dix heures. However quickly we walk, we
> shall not be there before ten o'clock.

Whoever

> Qui que vous soyez . . . whoever you may be . . .

Whatever (pronoun).

> Quoi que vous disiez . . . whatever you may say . . .

CHAPTER V

ADVERBS

Adverbs are words that qualify or modify the meaning of a verb. In a sentence like "she sings sweetly", the word "sweetly" is an adverb: it tells us something about the verb "sings". Adverbs may also describe adjectives or other adverbs. "She sings very sweetly": in this sentence "very" is an adverb describing "sweetly", and if we say "he is extremely patient", "extremely" is an adverb describing the adjective "patient".

Position of Adverbs

Adverbs do not vary and can be spelt in one way only. In French the adverb generally follows the verb, but may be put for greater emphasis at the beginning of the sentence.

Elle pleure bien souvent. She cries very often.
Bien souvent elle pleure. Very often she cries.

What we must never do in French is to put the adverb between the subject and the verb as we do in English: "She very often comes here." This must be either Elle vient ici bien souvent or Bien souvent elle vient ici in French.

In a compound tense a short adverb generally comes before the Past Participle:

Nous y sommes souvent allés. We often went there.

Formation of Adverbs from Adjectives

1. Most adverbs are formed by adding -ment to the feminine of the adjective:

frais, (f.) fraîche: fraîchement, freshly.
heureux, (f.) heureuse: heureusement, happily.

2. If the adjective ends in a vowel, one simply adds -ment.

hardi, bold: hardiment, boldly.

vrai, true: vraiment, truly.

3. If the adjective ends in -ent or -ant, change these endings to -emment and -amment. Ardent, ardemment, ardently; constant, constamment, constantly. (N.B. lent, slow, becomes lentement, slowly.)

Some common exceptions to the above rules are: gentil, gentiment, nicely; aveugle, aveuglément, blindly; confus, confusément, confusedly; énorme, énormément, enormously; précis, précisément, precisely; profond, profondément, profoundly.

Adjectives Used as Adverbs

As sometimes happens in English, some adjectives may be used as adverbs. "That smells *good*", "Buy *British*!", etc. French examples are aller droit, to go straight; voir rouge, to see red; coûter cher, to cost a lot; parler haut, to speak up; parler bas, to speak in a whisper; sentir bon, to smell good; sentir mauvais, to smell bad; travailler ferme, to work hard; travailler dur, to work hard; acheter français, to buy French (goods made in France); voir clair, to see clear (-ly).

Comparison of Adverbs

Adverbs are compared like adjectives with the help of plus, more, and le plus, most; moins, less, and le moins, least; aussi . . . que, as . . . as. Thus:

Positive.	Comparative.	Superlative.
vite, quickly	plus vite, more quickly	le plus vite, most quickly
	moins vite, less quickly	le moins vite, least quickly

Il marche vite. He walks quickly.

Il marche plus vite que vous. He walks more quickly than you.

C'est lui qui marche le plus vite. It is he who walks most quickly (the fastest).

Il marche aussi vite que vous. He walks as quickly as you.

Il ne marche pas si vite que vous. He does not walk so quickly as you.

Il marche moins vite que vous. He walks less quickly than you.

Irregular Comparison

peu, little	moins, less	le moins, least
beaucoup, much	plus, more	le plus, most
mal, badly	plus mal ⎫ pis ⎭ worse*	le plus mal ⎫ le pis ⎭ worst
bien, well	mieux, better	le mieux, best

Je mange peu mais ma femme mange moins que moi. I eat little but my wife eats less than I.

Il chante beaucoup, mais c'est son frère qui chante le plus. He sings a lot, but it is his brother who sings most.

PLUS and MOINS with a Numeral

After plus and moins, de is used instead of que before numerals or when there is no real comparison.

Il a moins de vingt livres dans sa maison. He has fewer than twenty books in his house.

Il a mangé plus d'un kilo de pommes. He has eaten more than a kilo of apples.

---

* pis is used nowadays only in certain expressions: tant pis pour moi, so much the worse for me; de mal en pis, from bad to worse.

Expletive NE after a Comparative

If there is a verb after a comparative, it has an expletive or untranslated ne before it.

Il mange plus que vous *ne* croyez. He eats more than you think.

The More . . . the Less . . .

Do not forget that in sentences like "The more he has, the more he wants"; "The less he works, the more he earns", the article is omitted in French:

Plus il a, plus il désire.
Moins il travaille, plus il gagne.

Adverbs of Affirmation—OUI and SI

There are two words for "yes": oui and si. Oui is more common; si being used only in a contradictory sense in answer to a negative question.

Vous allez faire cela? Oui! You are going to do that? Yes!

Vous n'allez pas faire cela? Si! You are not going to do that? Oh, yes, I am!

Note too je crois que oui, je pense que oui, I think so.

Adverbs of Negation—NON and NE . . . PAS

Negation is expressed by NON or by NE . . . PAS and a verb

Non is used to answer a question:

Vous aimez le café? Non! You like coffee? No!

Non is also used when the negative comes immediately before a word which is not a verb.

Non loin de la forêt je vois une chaumière. Not far from the forest I see a cottage.

Il est non seulement pauvre, mais aussi très malade. Not only is he poor, he is also very ill.

Neither (Either)

Non is also used with **plus** to express "neither" or "either" with a negative:

> **Mon frère ne vient pas non plus.** My brother isn't coming either.
>
> **Vous n'aimez pas le poivre? Moi non plus.** You don't like pepper? Neither do I.

Negation with a Verb

The usual negative used with a verb is **NE** (placed before the verb) and **PAS** (placed after the verb): **j'accepte**, I accept; **je n'accepte pas**, I'm not accepting. In compound tenses, the **PAS** comes before the Past Participle: **Il a parlé**, he spoke; **il n'a pas parlé**, he did not speak.

Similar in use are **ne . . . point**, not at all; **ne . . . plus**, no more, no longer; **ne . . . que**, only; **ne . . . guère**, scarcely; **ne . . . jamais**, never; **ne . . . ni . . . ni**, neither . . . nor; **ne . . . nulle part**, nowhere; **ne . . . personne**, nobody; **ne . . . rien**, nothing; **ne . . . aucun, ne . . . nul**, not . . . any.

> **Je n'ai plus de pain.** I have no more bread.
>
> **Il ne sort que le soir.** He only* goes out in the evening.
>
> **Nous n'allons jamais au cinéma.** We never go to the cinema.
>
> **Vous n'avez ni plume ni encre.** You have neither pen nor ink.
>
> **Il n'a rien dit.** He said nothing.
>
> **Vous n'avez** $\left.\begin{matrix}\text{aucune}\\\text{nulle}\end{matrix}\right\}$ **idée.** You have $\left\{\begin{matrix}\text{not any}\\\text{no}\end{matrix}\right.$ idea.
>
> **Nous n'avons vu personne.** We have seen nobody.

* "Only" is rather difficult. When "only" describes a verb in sentences like "he only laughs at me", "he doesn't work, he only gives advice", we add the verb **faire**: **il ne fait que rire de moi; il ne travaille pas, il ne fait que conseiller.** "Not only" with a verb may be translated by **ne . . . pas seulement**:

> **Il n'est pas seulement acteur, il est aussi auteur.** He is not only an actor, he is also an author.

In compound tenses **personne** comes after the Past Participle; **point, plus, guère, jamais, rien** come before it.

> **Ils n'avaient rencontré personne en route.** They had met no one on the way.
>
> **Elle n'est jamais allée en France.** She has never been to France.
>
> **Il n'avait rien fait.** He had done nothing.

Que, ni, aucun, nul come before the word that they modify:

> **Il n'y est resté *qu'*un instant.** He stayed there a moment only.
>
> **Elle n'a fait *aucune* attention à moi.** She paid no attention to me.

Of course, when the sentence begins with the negative, *nothing, nobody, never*, etc., the order of the words is similar to that in the corresponding English sentence:

> Nobody is there. **Personne n'est là.**
>
> Not a single soldier escaped. **Pas un seul soldat n'échappa.**

Two negatives may combine:

> **Il n'en a jamais rien dit.** He never said anything about it.

When the verb is not expressed, the **ne** is left out:

> **Qu'avez-vous fait? Rien!** What did you do? Nothing!
>
> **A-t-il été à Nice? Jamais.** Has he been to Nice? Never.

Pas may be omitted with the verbs **pouvoir, oser, savoir** and **cesser**:

> **Ils n'osèrent entrer.** They dared not enter.
>
> **Je ne sais si vous pouvez y aller.** I don't know if you can go there.
>
> **Il ne cessa de pleurer.** He did not stop crying.

TOUT (Quite, Completely)

This adverb, unlike others, can change. When it stands before a feminine adjective beginning with a *consonant* or *h aspirate*, it agrees with the noun like an adjective.

Elle est *toute* contente. She is quite pleased.

but Elle est *tout* étonnée. She is quite astonished.

Elles sont *toutes* confuses. They are quite confused.

but Ils sont *tout* heureux. They are quite happy.

Marie était *toute* honteuse (h aspirate). Mary was quite ashamed.

but Ils ont été *tout* surpris. They have been quite surprised.

C'est une *tout* autre proposition. It's quite a different proposition.

[If you find this too difficult, you may use, instead of tout, the adverb tout à fait, which means more or less the same thing and which never changes.]

Tout may also be used before an adjective in the sense of "however" (though).

Tout intelligents qu'ils sont, ils ne réussiront pas.
However intelligent they are ⎫
Intelligent though they may be ⎭ , they will not succeed.

COMME and COMMENT

Both can mean "how".

Comment is either an exclamation meaning "What!" or "What?"

Comment! Il a osé venir chez moi. What! He dared to come to my house.

Quel est le chemin le plus court? Comment? Which is the shortest way? What (did you say)?

or at the beginning of an interrogative sentence means "how?"

Comment expliquez-vous cela? How do you explain that?

Comme, which can also mean "like" or "as" (fort comme un taureau, strong as a bull), may also introduce a sentence but not an interrogative one.

> Comme elle est belle! How beautiful she is!
> Comme il fait beau! How fine the weather is!

Notice the word order in these sentences.

PLUTÔT AND PLUS TÔT

Plutôt means "rather".

> Plutôt souffrir que mourir! Rather suffer than die!

Plus tôt means "earlier".

> Deux jours plus tôt. Two days earlier.

ASSEZ, Enough, Rather, Fairly, Quite

Ce livre me semble assez intéressant. This book seems rather } interesting.
quite }

Il est assez* grand pour voyager tout seul. He is big enough to travel on his own.

Expressions of Quantity

Assez, enough; beaucoup, much, many, a lot; tant, so much, so many; autant, as much, as many; trop, too much, too many; combien, how much, how many; peu, little, few; un peu, a little; plus, more; moins, less, fewer; pas mal, quite a lot (familiar), are followed by de when standing before a noun: assez de pain, enough bread; beaucoup de choses, a lot of things; tant de monde, so many people; trop de sucre, too much sugar; un peu de musique, a little music; peu de gens, few people.

---

* A similar construction is used with trop (too):

> Il n'est jamais trop tard, pour bien faire. It is never too late to do good.

Bien, also meaning "many, a lot", is followed by **des: bien des fois,** many times; so too is **la plupart,** most, the majority: **la plupart des hommes,** most (of the) men.

Encore, more, is followed by **du (de la, de l', des):**

> **Encore du pain, s'il vous plaît.** Some more bread, please.

Such (as an Adverb)

"Such" in English may be used as an adjective or an adverb. In French we have different words. In expressions like "such a man", "such books", "such" is an adjective and is rendered by **tel (telle, tels, telles): un tel homme, de tels livres.** When, however, we write "such a good man", "such interesting books", "such" in these cases is an adverb describing the adjectives "good" and "interesting" and is translated by **tellement** or **si.** Such a good book, **un si bon livre** or **un livre tellement bon;** such interesting films, **des films si intéressants** or **des films tellement intéressants.**

PEUT-ÊTRE, Perhaps

If **peut-être** is put at the beginning of the sentence it is followed by inversion of the verb and pronoun.

> **Il viendra peut-être demain.** He will come tomorrow perhaps.

but

> **Peut-être viendra-t-il demain.** Perhaps he will come tomorrow.

By adding **que** after **peut-être,** one can avoid inversion:

> **Peut-être qu'il viendra demain.**

AUSSI, and so

Aussi has a similar construction after it.

> **Elle était fatiguée; aussi se coucha-t-elle.** She was tired; (and) so she went to bed.

Aussi placed after a verb means "also", "too".

Elle va venir, elle aussi. She is coming also.

QUELQUE

Quelque may be used as an adverb:

Elle a quelque soixante ans. She is some sixty years old (about sixty).

Quelque vite que vous couriez . . . However quickly you may run . . .

DAVANTAGE, More

Davantage is used instead of **plus** when it stands on its own at the end of a clause.

Il a peu d'argent, vous en avez davantage. He has little money, you have more.

If anything is added, **plus** must be employed:

Il a peu d'argent, vous en avez plus que lui. He has little money, you have more than he.

DESSUS, DESSOUS, DEDANS, DEHORS

Do not confuse **dessus**, on it; **dessous**, under it; **dedans**, in it; **dehors**, outside, with the corresponding prepositions **sur**, on; **sous**, under; **dans**, in; **hors**, outside.

Les livres sont sur la table: ils sont dessus. The books are on the table: they are on it (on top).

Les fruits sont dans le buffet: ils sont dedans. The fruits are in the sideboard: they are in it (inside).

In this connection we must also mention the adverbs **là-dedans**, in there, within; **là-dehors**, outside; **là-dessous**, underneath; **là-dessus**, thereon, thereupon.

Là-dessus, elle est partie. Thereupon she went away.

Adverbs of Time

Avant-hier, the day before yesterday; **hier,** yesterday; **aujourd'hui,** today; **demain,** tomorrow; **après-demain,** the day after tomorrow, are all adverbs.

> **Demain il donne sa démission.** Tomorrow he is resigning.

The corresponding nouns are **l'avant-veille,** two days previously; **la veille,** the day before, the eve; **ce jour-là,** that day; **le lendemain,** the next day; **le surlendemain,** two days later.

> **La veille de Noël,** Christmas Eve
> **Le lendemain du bal, il se sentait bien fatigué.** The day after the dance he felt very tired.

CHAPTER VI

PRONOUNS

Pronouns are words that can replace nouns in a sentence. Instead of *"Mrs. Jones* is still here", we can use a pronoun to write *"She* is still here". Similarly for "I water *the plants*", we may say "I water *them*"; for "I talk to *the Director*", "I talk *to him*"; for "we go *to Paris*", "we go *there*".

Here is a reference table of Personal Pronouns:

Persons	Subject	Direct Object	Indirect Object	Reflexive (Direct and Indirect)	Disjunctive
Singular					
1st	je, I	me, me	me, to me	me, (to) myself	moi
2nd	tu, thou	te, thee	te, to thee	te, (to) thyself	toi
3rd Masc.	il, he, it	le, him, it	lui, to him	se, (to) himself	lui (soi)
3rd Fem.	elle, she, it	la, her, it	lui, to her	se, (to) herself	elle
Plural					
1st	nous, we	nous, us	nous, to us	nous, (to) ourselves	nous
2nd	vous, you	vous, you	vous, to you	vous, (to) yourself, yourselves	vous
3rd Masc.	ils, they	les, them	leur, to them	se, (to) themselves	eux
3rd Fem.	elles, they	les, them	leur, to them	se, (to) themselves	elles

The first type of pronouns we meet are those used as Subjects of verbs:

je donne, *I* give	*nous* donnons, *we* give
tu donnes, *thou* givest	*vous* donnez, *you* give
il donne, *he* (*it*) gives	*ils* donnent, *they* give
elle donne, *she* (*it*) gives	*elles* donnent, *they* give

1. Tu is used in French instead of **vous** when speaking to a child, a relative, a close friend or an animal. Its use is tending to spread, like Christian names in this country, with the increasing "familiarity" of modern times.

2. Il and Elle can also refer to things and mean "it".

Où est mon chapeau? Il est sur la table. Where is my hat? It is on the table.

3. Je becomes j' before a vowel or mute h: j'ai, j'habite, etc., but not when used interrogatively:

Puis-je entrer? May I come in?

OBJECT PRONOUNS (DIRECT AND INDIRECT OBJECTS)

These pronouns too are used with verbs and may be Direct or Indirect Objects.

Direct Objects.	Indirect Objects.
il *me* voit, he sees *me*	elle *me* parle, she speaks *to me*
il *te* voit, he sees *thee*	elle *te* parle, she speaks *to thee*
il *le* voit, he sees *him* (*it*)	elle *lui* parle, she speaks *to him*
il *la* voit, he sees *her* (*it*)	elle *lui* parle, she speaks *to her*
il *nous* voit, he sees *us*	elle *nous* parle, she speaks *to us*
il *vous* voit, he sees *you*	elle *vous* parle, she speaks *to you*
il *les* voit, he sees *them*	elle *leur* parle, she speaks *to them*

REFLEXIVE PRONOUNS (DIRECT AND INDIRECT OBJECTS)

Direct Object.	Indirect Object.
je *me* lave, I wash *myself*	je *me* dis, I say *to myself*
tu *te* laves, thou washes *thyself*	tu *te* dis, thou sayest *to thyself*
il *se* lave, he washes *himself*	il *se* dit, he says *to himself*
elle *se* lave, she washes *herself*	elle *se* dit, she says *to herself*
nous *nous* lavons, we wash *ourselves*	nous *nous* disons, we say *to ourselves*
vous *vous* lavez, you wash { *yourself* *yourselves*	vous *vous* dites, you say to { *yourself* *yourselves*
ils *se* lavent, they wash *themselves*	ils *se* disent, they say *to themselves*
elles *se* lavent, they wash *themselves*	elles *se* disent, they say *to themselves*

Uses of the Above Pronouns

1. Le, la, les may refer to things as well as to people, depending on the gender of the noun.

> Où est ma plume? Je ne peux pas *la* trouver. Where is my pen? I cannot find it.

2. Le, la, les are often used in French to complete the sense of a verb when the English equivalent is not needed:

> Êtes-vous le père de cet enfant? Je *le* suis. Are you the father of this child? I am (him).
> Savez-vous qu'il est déjà arrivé? Je *le* sais. Do you know that he has already arrived? I know (it).
> Vous y allez aussi? Je *le* crois. Are you going too? I think (so).

3. The Indirect Object is used after dire, to say, to tell; demander, to ask; ordonner, to order, etc.

> Je *lui* ai dit de le faire. I told him to do so.
> Nous *leur* avons demandé de venir. We asked them to come.

Y, there, to it, to them

Another important pronoun is Y, meaning "there", "to it", "to them". It stands instead of a thing or things, not for a person or persons: it is used for *à and a noun.*

> Êtes-vous allé *à Paris*? J'*y* vais cet été. Have you been to Paris? I'm going there this summer.
> Elle pense déjà *à ses vacances.* She is already thinking of (lit. "to") her holidays.
> Elle *y* pense déjà. She is already thinking of (lit. "to") them.

Je ne prête pas attention *à son discours.* I pay no attention to his speech.

Je n'*y* prête pas attention. I pay no attention to it.

EN, of it, of them, some, any

En, as you see, has many meanings. It stands instead of *de and a noun.*

Combien *de beurre* désirez-vous? How much butter do you want?

J'*en* désire un kilo. I want a kilo (of it).

Combien *de frères* avez-vous? How many brothers have you?

J'*en* ai quatre. I have four (of them).

Avez-vous *des bonbons?* Have you any sweets?

Oui j'*en* ai. Yes I have (some).

Non, je n'*en* ai pas. No, I haven't (any).

Êtes-vous content *de mon travail?* Are you pleased with (lit. "of") my work?

Oui, j'*en* suis bien content. Yes, I'm very pleased (with it).

Notice that en must be used in French where in English the corresponding pronoun may be omitted.

Position of the Object Pronouns

(*a*) These object pronouns are placed immediately before a verb except in the Imperative Affirmative:

Il *me* voit. He sees me.

Il ne *la* voit pas. He does not see her.

Il ne *lui* a pas parlé. He did not speak to her. (The Pronoun is placed before the auxiliary verb in compound tenses.)

Elle n'*y* est jamais allée. She never went there.
Les avez-vous vus à la foire? Did you see them at the fair?
Ne *le* regardez pas! Don't look at it!
N'*en* mangeons pas! Let us not eat any!

(*b*) In the Imperative Affirmative, the Pronouns come immediately after the verb and are joined to it by hyphens. **Me** and **te** change to **MOI** and **TOI**.

Allez-y! Go there!
Lavez-vous! Wash yourself!
Regardez-moi! Look at me!
Regarde-toi! Look at thyself!
Dépêchons-nous! Let us hurry (ourselves)!

Do not forget that in the Imperative *Negative*, the pronouns take their normal position *before* the verb:

N'y allez pas! Don't go there!
Ne vous lavez pas! Do not wash yourself!
Ne me regardez pas! Do not look at me!
Ne te regarde pas! Don't look at thyself!
Ne nous dépêchons pas! Let us not hurry (ourselves)!

(*c*) The pronouns come before **voici** and **voilà**.

Me voici. Here I am.
Le voilà. There he is.
Nous voici. Here we are.

(*d*) When two verbs come together, the pronoun precedes the verb which governs it:

Il vient *me* voir ce matin. He is coming to see me this morning.
Vous avez essayé de *l'*aider. You have tried to help him.

Order of the Object Pronouns

If we have two or more pronouns, in which order are they to be written? If the pronouns come *before* the verb the order of precedence is:

1	2	3	4	5
me te se nous vous	le la les	lui leur	y	en

Try to learn by heart this string of pronouns: **me, te, se, nous, vous, le, la, les, lui, leur, y, en.** If you know this and you have to decide whether **me** or **le** comes first, or choose between **lui** and **en**, you will make no mistakes.

Thus:

Elle *me l'*envoie. She sends it to me.

Vous *lui en* donnez. You give some to him.

Nous *l'y* avons cherché. We looked for him there.

If you cannot remember the above list, try this rule: 1–2–3–Direct–Indirect–Y–EN. Thus a 1st Person (**me** or **nous**) will come before a 2nd Person (**te** or **vous**), which in turn will precede a 3rd (**le, la, les, lui, leur**). If the two pronouns are both in the 3rd Person, then the Direct Object (**le, la, les**) will have precedence over the Indirect (**lui, leur**). **Y** and **en** always come last in that order. **Y EN** sounds something like Hee Haw! so that even a donkey knows that **Y** comes before **EN**!

What happens when the pronouns come *after* the verb (i.e., in the Imperative Affirmative)? The order is much as it is in English: "Send them to me!" "Give it to him". The Direct Object comes before the Indirect with once again **y** and **en** bringing up the rear. Thus: 1. Direct Object, 2. Indirect Object, 3. **y**, 4. **en.**

Envoyez-les-moi! Send them to me!
Donnez-le-lui! Give it to him!

Before **y** and **en**, **moi** and **toi** become **m'** and **t'**:

Donnez-m'en! Give me some!
Va-t'en! Go away!

DISJUNCTIVE PRONOUNS

These are **moi, toi, lui, elle, nous, vous, eux, elles,** together with **soi.** As their name implies, these pronouns are used when the pronoun is not linked with a verb.

We find them:

1. After a preposition: **avec moi**, with me; **sans toi**, without thee; **derrière lui**, behind him; **avant elle**, before her; **après vous**, after you; **près d'eux**, near them; **chez elles**, to their house.

2. Standing alone in answer to a question or in an exclamation together with an infinitive:

Qui donc a parlé? Who spoke then?
Moi. Me (*or better* I did).

Moi, faire cela! I (Me) do that!
Jamais! Never!

3. After a comparative:

Elle est plus petite que lui. She is shorter than he.

4. Showing emphasis when combined with a subject pronoun or with **même, seul, aussi**:

Eux, ils sont innocents. *They* are innocent.
Lui seul ose le faire. He alone dares do it.
Moi aussi, je veux y aller. I too want to go there.
Je le ferai moi-même. I shall do it myself.

5. After c'est, ce sont: c'est moi, c'est toi, c'est lui, c'est elle, c'est nous, c'est vous *but* ce sont eux, ce sont elles, it is I, it is thou, it is he, etc.

>C'est lui qui est arrivé le premier. It's he who came in first.

6. When the subject of the verb is a double one:

>Mon frère et moi, nous y allons souvent. My brother and I often go there.
>Vous et moi, nous sommes faits pour nous entendre. You and I are made to understand each other.

7. After verbs of motion and the verb penser:

>Il courut à moi. He ran to me.
>Il pensait à eux. He was thinking of them.

8. Expressing possession with the verb être:

>Ce livre est à lui. This book belongs to him.

9. After reflexive verbs:

>Elle s'est approchée de moi. She approached me.
>Je me suis fié à lui. I trusted myself to him.

10. When the direct object pronoun is not in the 3rd Person. In that case a disjunctive pronoun is used for the indirect object:

>Je le lui présente. I introduce him to her.
>*but*
>Je vous présente à elle. I introduce you to her.
>Je me présente à eux. I introduce myself to them.

Soi

What about soi? Soi is used when the subject is an indefinite pronoun like chacun, each one; tout le monde, everybody; personne, nobody; on, one.

>Chacun pour soi. Every man for himself.
>On a souvent besoin d'un plus petit que soi. One often needs someone smaller than oneself.

DEMONSTRATIVE PRONOUNS

celui (masc.), the one	celle (fem.), the one
ceux (masc.), the ones	celles (fem.), the ones

This is a most important pronoun with many uses:

1. **Mon crayon et celui de mon frère.** My pencil and my brother's (the one of my brother).

   Ma chambre et celle de mon oncle. My bedroom and my uncle's (the one of my uncle).

   Mes livres et ceux de votre tante. My books and your aunt's (the ones of your aunt).

   Je préfère mes fleurs à celles de mon voisin. I prefer my flowers to those (the ones) of my neighbour (to my neighbour's).

   Tous ceux qui viennent. All (those, the ones) who come.

   Celui qui hésite est perdu. He (the one) who hesitates, is lost.

2. Used in conjunction with -ci (here), -là (there): thus:

   celui-ci (masc.), the one here, this one, this
   celle-là (fem.), the one there, that one, that
   ceux-là (masc. plur.), the ones there, those ones, those
   celles-ci (fem. plur.), the ones here, these ones, these
   J'aime les deux tableaux, mais celui-ci est plus beau que celui-là. I like both pictures, but this (one) is finer than that (one).

Celui-ci (celle-ci) has also the sense of "the latter"; celui-là (celle-là) the meaning of "the former".

   Corneille et La Fontaine vivaient au dix-septième siècle; celui-là était dramaturge, celui-ci était fabuliste. Corneille and La Fontaine lived in the seventeenth century; the former was a dramatist, the latter a fabulist.

CECI, this; CELA, * that

Ceci and cela have only one form each. They are used when we are neither speaking of persons nor referring to particular nouns already mentioned. Ceci refers to something we are about to mention, cela to something already said.

Écoutez ceci, mon ami! Listen to this, my friend!

Mentir à son père! Je n'aime pas cela! Lie to one's father! I don't like that!

When cela is found with the verb être it is divided up into ce and là:

Ce n'est pas là une belle action. That is not a nice deed.

RELATIVE PRONOUNS

Relative pronouns are words like "who","which","that", "whose", which join two clauses together to make a longer sentence.

This is the house *that* Jack built.

She is the girl *who* appeared on television.

The man *whose* son won a "blue" at Cambridge is standing next to the vicar.

Here's the pen with *which* he wrote the letter.

The first point to note is that the Relative Pronoun must never be left out in French. "The man I saw yesterday" may sound correct in English, but before you can translate it into French, you must rewrite it as "The man *whom* I saw yesterday". Secondly, where we may use in English a phrase such as "The pen I am writing with", we must recast it to "The pen *with which* I am writing" before turning it into French.

To make this as simple as possible, you would be wise to realise that there are really two main kinds of sentences in which Relative Pronouns appear:

* In conversation, cela is nearly always shortened to ça.

(1) *Relative Pronouns Used with Prepositions*

When the Relative Pronoun is used with a Preposition (i.e., with a word like "to", "of", "at", "on", "with", etc.).

> The man *with whom* you were speaking is my uncle.
> The boy *to whom* he is writing is ill.
> The chair *on which* you were sitting is broken.
> The houses *in which* they lived were very old.

In cases like this, we use QUI if we are referring to persons and LEQUEL, LAQUELLE, LESQUELS, LESQUELLES for things.* Thus the above sentences would be translated:

> L'homme avec *qui* vous parliez est mon oncle.
> Le garçon à *qui* il écrit est malade.
> La chaise sur *laquelle* vous étiez assis est cassée.
> Les maisons dans *lesquelles* ils demeuraient étaient très vieilles.

The prepositions de and à combine with lequel, laquelle, lesquels, lesquelles to form:

> with de: duquel, de laquelle, desquels, desquelles
> with à: auquel, à laquelle, auxquels, auxquelles

> Le chien au courage duquel je dois la vie . . . The dog to whose courage (the courage of which) I owe my life . . .
> La rue au coin de laquelle elle demeure . . . The street at the corner of which she lives . . .
> Le livre auquel il faisait allusion . . . The book to which he was alluding . . .

DONT, of whom, of which, whose.

However, if the Relative Pronoun stands next to its antecedent (the noun to which it refers) it is better to use

---

* After parmi (among) and entre (between) we use lequel, etc., even of persons:

> Les prisonniers parmi lesquels il se trouvait. The prisoners amongst whom he found himself.

the invariable DONT instead of de qui, duquel, de laquelle, desquels or desquelles.

> Les livres dont vous parlez . . . The books of which you speak . . .
>
> L'homme dont le fils mourut en Algérie . . . The man whose (of whom the) son died in Algeria . . .
>
> La femme dont il connaissait le frère . . . The woman whose brother he knew (of whom he knew the brother) . . .
>
> Les journaux dont il lisait les articles . . . The newspapers whose articles he read (of which he read the articles) . . .

Notice the word-order after DONT:

When the Relative Pronoun does not immediately follow its antecedent, DONT may not be used. We then have to employ qui or lequel, etc.

> Cet homme (antecedent) à la bonté de qui (relative pronoun) je me fie . . . This man in the goodness of whom I trust . . .
>
> La maison dans le jardin de laquelle j'aime me reposer . . . The house in the garden of which (in whose garden) I like to rest . . .

Quoi (what) may also serve as a relative pronoun in conjunction with a preposition when referring to something vague and indeterminate:

> Trouvez-moi quelque chose sur quoi écrire. Find me something on which to write.
>
> Il se reposa un moment: après quoi il se remit à travailler. He rested for a moment: after which he started to work again.

Où (where) may also replace with advantage dans lequel or auquel, etc.:

> La maison où (or dans laquelle) je demeure . . . The house where (in which) I live . . .

La ville d'où (or de laquelle) il vient . . . The town from
which he comes (where he comes from).

(2) *Relative Pronouns Used without Prepositions*

In this case we use QUI, if the pronoun is the subject of
the following verb and QUE (QU' before a vowel or mute h)
if it is the object.

La lettre *qui* est sur la table . . . The letter which is on
the table . . .

La lettre *que* vous écrivez . . . The letter which you are
writing . . .

Le jeune homme *qui* passe devant la maison . . . The
young man who passes the house . . .

Les personnes *que* je vois tous les jours . . . The people
that I see every day . . .

The student is often puzzled when a French writer reverses
the normal order of words in the sentence after que:

J'ai remarqué l'effet que produisit ce discours. I
noticed the effect which this speech produced.

La maison qu'ont bâtie mes aïeux . . . The house which
my ancestors built . . .

This inversion is frequent in this type of sentence, and the
student must be on his guard.

CE QUI, CE QUE, CE DONT

"What" is expressed by ce qui or ce que: ce qui if the pronoun is the subject of the subsequent verb, ce que if it is
the object:

Dites-moi ce qui vous intéresse. Tell me what interests
you.

Dites-moi ce que vous préférez. Tell me what you
prefer.

Racontez-moi ce dont il vous parlait. Tell me what he
was speaking to you about (that of which he was
speaking).

TOUT CE QUI, TOUT CE QUE

"All that", "everything" is tout ce qui (subject), or tout ce que (object).

Tout ce qui brille n'est pas or. All that glitters is not gold.

Je sais tout ce que vous avez fait. I know everything (that) you have done.

POSSESSIVE PRONOUNS

	Masc. Sing.	Fem. Sing.	Masc. Plur.	Fem. Plur.
mine	le mien	la mienne	les miens	les miennes
thine	le tien	la tienne	les tiens	les tiennes
his	le sien	la sienne	les siens	les siennes
hers	le sien	la sienne	les siens	les siennes
ours	le nôtre	la nôtre	les nôtres	les nôtres
yours	le vôtre	la vôtre	les vôtres	les vôtres
theirs	le leur	la leur	les leurs	les leurs

The gender of the Possessive Pronoun depends not on the gender of the owner but on that of the article possessed. Thus cette montre est la sienne could mean either "this watch is his" or "this watch is hers". A man talking of his house (la maison) might say, La mienne est plus grande que la vôtre. A woman referring to a book (le livre) may say, Le mien n'est pas très intéressant. Mine is not very interesting.

In the 3rd Person, when there is a need to distinguish between "his" and "hers" one says le sien à lui, la sienne à lui (his); le sien à elle, la sienne à elle (hers).

Of course, if you just want to express possession one may use the disjunctive pronouns:

Ce crayon est à lui. This pencil is his.

Ce livre est à moi is much more common than Ce livre est le mien.

INTERROGATIVE PRONOUNS
Who? Whom?

(*a*) As subject of a sentence, "who?" is expressed by Qui? or Qui est-ce qui?

> Qui est à la porte? Who is at the door?

or

> Qui est-ce qui est à la porte? Who is it who is at the door.

(*b*) "Whom?" as object of a verb is "qui?" or "qui est-ce que?"

> Qui voyez-vous? Whom do you see?
> Qui est-ce que vous voyez? Who is it that you see?

(*c*) "Whom" with a preposition is expressed by qui.

> À qui parliez-vous? To whom were you speaking?

À qui is also used to inquire about ownership.

À qui est ce livre? { Whose book is this?
                     { To whom does this book belong?

Ce livre est à moi. This book { is mine.
                              { belongs to me.

What? (Subject or Object)

(*a*) "What?" as subject of a sentence is Qu'est-ce qui?

Qu'est-ce qui est arrivé? { What has happened?
                          { What is it that has
                          {   happened?

(*b*) "What?" as object is que? or qu'est-ce que?

> Que voyez-vous? What do you see?
> Qu'est-ce que vous voyez? What is it that you see?

Note too:

Qu'est-ce?   } What is it?
Qu'est-ce que c'est?   } (What is it that it is?)
Qu'est-ce que c'est que cela? What is that?

C'est un bouton. It's a button.
Que faire? What's to be done?
Qu'importe? What does it matter?

Que may also be used with de as an exclamation with the sense of "What a lot of!"

Que d'eau! What a lot of water!

(c) "What?" (with a preposition). "What?" after a preposition is translated by "quoi".

De quoi avez-vous parlé? What did you talk about?
Avec quoi l'a-t-il fait? What did he do it with?
À quoi pensiez-vous? What were you thinking of?

In French the preposition must not end the sentence, but must be carried forward to join with quoi: *of what, with what,* etc.

Quoi may also stand on its own to show surprise or indignation:

Quoi! vous êtes encore là! What! you are still there!

In familiar and impolite language it is used when one has not heard another person's remark.

Marie, viens ici tout de suite! Marie, come here at once!
Quoi? What (did you say)?

Quoi is also found with de and an adjective:

Quoi de nouveau? What news?
Quoi d'autre? What else?
Quoi de plus beau que cela? What could be finer than that?

Which? or Which one(s)?

Lequel (m.), laquelle (f.), lesquels (m. pl.), lesquelles (f. pl.), contracted with à and de to auquel, à laquelle, auxquel(le)s, duquel, de laquelle, desquel(le)s, is another interrogative pronoun.

Lequel de ces livres allez-vous prendre? Which (one) of these books are you going to take?

Auquel des professeurs a-t-il parlé? To which of the masters has he spoken?

As you can see from these examples, **lequel** is used to find out a person's choice.

INDEFINITE PRONOUNS

There are many of these. Below you will find a list together with their meanings and examples of their use:

quelqu'un(e), someone, somebody

Quelqu'un est entré dans cette chambre. Someone has entered this room.

quelques-uns, quelques-unes, some (people)

quelques-uns d'entre nous, some of us

quelque chose, something (masculine)

Cela me fait quelque chose! That does something to me!

J'ai vu quelque chose à la fenêtre. I saw something at the window.

Quelque chose de nouveau, something new

Quelque chose, whatever (thing) (f.)

Quelque chose qu'il ait faite . . . Whatever (thing) he has done . . .

grand'chose, much (nearly always after pas)

Les femmes ne valent pas grand'chose, les hommes ne valent rien du tout! Women aren't worth much, men are worth nothing at all!

autre chose, something else

Voudriez-vous voir autre chose, monsieur? Would you like to see something else?

peu de chose, little

Il a peu de chose de neuf à vous dire. He has little to tell you that is new.

on, one, they, you, etc. (often used to avoid Passive Voice)

On dit qu'il va mieux. It is said ⎱ that he is getting
                     They say ⎰   better.

Ici on parle français. Here they speak French. French
    is spoken here.

On doit manger pour vivre. One must eat to live.

In familiar language, **on** is often used for **je, nous** or **vous.**

Comment va-t-on? How are you?
On n'est pas fier. I'm not fussy.
On sort ce soir? Shall we go out tonight?

chacun, each one, everyone

chacun de vous, everyone of you
chacun son métier, each man (to) his trade

quiconque, whoever, whosoever

Quiconque fera cela, s'exposera à de grands dangers.
    Whoever does that will run great dangers.

n'importe qui, anybody (you like) (lit. no matter who)

N'importe qui pourrait le faire! Anybody could do it!

n'importe quoi, anything (you like) (lit. no matter what)

Il mange n'importe quoi! He eats anything!

n'importe où, anywhere

Pour gagner ma vie, j'irais n'importe où. To earn my
    living, I would go anywhere.

je ne sais qui, somebody or other (lit. I don't know who)

Je ne sais qui me l'a dit. Somebody or other told me.

je ne sais quoi, something or other

**Il y a un je ne sais quoi dans sa manière de parler qui
    me choque.** There's something in his way of speaking
    which shocks me.

tout, all, everything

> **Tout est perdu.** All is lost.
> **Nous avons tout vu.** We saw everything.
> **Tout ce que vous voyez ici m'appartient.** Everything you see here belongs to me.

tous, all (plural); **toutes**

> **Ils sont tous venus.** They all came.
> **Nous étions** $\begin{Bmatrix} \text{toutes} \\ \text{tous} \end{Bmatrix}$ **là.** All of us were there.

Notice that **tous** and **toutes** come immediately after the verb.

tous (toutes) les deux, both

> **Ils sont morts tous les deux.** Both of them died.

tout le monde, everyone, everybody

> **Tout le monde le connaît.** Everyone knows him.

plusieurs, several

> **Plusieurs d'entre eux s'échappèrent.** Several of them escaped.

l'un ... l'autre, one ... the other

> **Il a deux fils: l'un est brun, l'autre est blond.** He has two sons: one is dark, the other is fair.

l'un l'autre, l'un à l'autre (of two people); **les uns les autres, les uns aux autres** (of more than two people) are often used with reflexive verbs to remove ambiguity.

> **Ils s'aiment l'un l'autre.** They love each other.
> (**Ils s'aiment** on its own might mean "they love themselves".)
> **Les femmes se disaient les unes aux autres ...** The women were saying to each other ...

se, each other, one another

> Ils se détestent l'un l'autre. They hate each other.
> Ils se jetèrent des cailloux les uns aux autres. They threw stones at each other.

"It" as Subject of a Verb

1. To tell the time, use **il.**

> Il est une heure. It is one o'clock.

2. To describe weather, use **il.**

> Il fait du vent. It is windy.

3. To refer to a noun just mentioned, use **il** or **elle** according to the gender.

> Où est mon chapeau? Where is my hat?
> Il est sur la table. It is on the table.
> Où est l'église? Where is the church?
> Elle est près de la gare. It is near the station.

4. To explain what a thing is or who a person is, use **c'est.**

> Qu'est-ce? What is it?
> C'est un bouton. It is a button.
> Qui est-ce? Who is it?
> C'est un de mes cousins. It (he) is one of my cousins.

5. Before disjunctive pronouns use **c'est** or **ce sont.**

> C'est moi. It is I (me).
> C'est vous. It is you.

"It Is" (with an Adjective)

"It is dangerous", "it is pleasant", etc.

1. When the main part of the sentence comes later, use **il est:**

> Il m'est difficile d'accepter sa proposition. It is difficult for me to accept his proposal.

2. When the main part of the sentence precedes, use c'est:

> Partir avant l'aube? C'est possible. Leave before dawn? It's possible.

This rule does not apply to adjectives etc. of emotion:

> C'est dommage de le voir si malade. It's a pity to see him so ill.
> C'est affreux qu'elle soit obligée de mendier. It's awful that she should be forced to beg.

"He Is", "She Is", "They Are"

Il est and c'est can both mean "he is"; elle est and c'est, "she is": the plurals of il est, elle est are ils sont, elles sont, c'est becomes ce sont.

Il est. Elle est

Use il est or elle est when the verb is followed by an adjective or a preposition.

> Elle est très sévère. She is very strict.
> Il est dans la cuisine. He is in the kitchen.
> Ils sont tous en vacances. They are all on holidays.

Il est and elle est may be used also when followed immediately by a noun showing nationality, profession, religion etc.

> Il est Anglais. He is an Englishman.
> Elle est institutrice. She is a schoolmistress.
> Mon frère? Il est catholique. My brother? He is a Catholic.

(One may also say: C'est un Anglais. He is an Englishman. C'est une institutrice. She is a schoolmistress, etc. But in this case the noun is preceded by an indefinite article.)

C'est

We put c'est (plural ce sont) for "he is", "she is" when it is followed by a noun accompanied by an article or adjective.

C'est une très bonne institutrice. She is a very good
   schoolmistress.

C'est mon cousin. He is my cousin.

Ce sont des amis. They are friends.

C'est may also serve to emphasise a particular part of the
sentence:

C'est moi qui suis arrivé le premier. It was I who came
   in first.

C'est à Londres que nous allons passer nos vacances.
   It's in London that we are going to spend our holidays.

"There" (with Impersonal Verbs)

Il can also have the sense of "there" when used before an
Impersonal Verb.

Il ne me reste que cent francs. {
   There remains to me
   only a hundred
   francs.
   I have only a hundred
   francs left.
}

Il arriva un accident. {
   There happened an accident.
   An accident happened.
}

Il était une fois une bergère. } There was once upon a
Il y avait une fois une bergère. } time a shepherdess.

CHAPTER VII

PREPOSITIONS

Prepositions are words which show the relationship between someone or something and another person or thing. Prepositions can be simple (i.e., consisting of one word) like **avec**, with, or compound like **au lieu de**, instead of.

Simple Prepositions

Here is a list of common simple prepositions:

à, at or to
après, after
avant, before (of time or order)
avec, with (accompanied by)
chez, at, to the house of
comme, like
contre, against
dans, in, into, inside
de, of, from
depuis, since (of time)
devant, in front of (place)
en, in
entre, between, among (two objects)
envers, towards (of emotions)

environ, about (with numbers)
excepté, except
malgré, in spite of
outre, besides
par, by, through
parmi, among
pendant, during
pour, for, in order to
sans, without
sauf, except
selon, according to
sous, under(neath)
sur, on, upon
vers, towards; about (of time)

Compound Prepositions

Here are some compound prepositions:

à cause de, because of
à côté de, beside, alongside of
à travers } through, across
au travers de }
au dessous de, below
au dessus de, above
au lieu de, instead of
au milieu de, in the middle of
auprès de, near, compared with

au sujet de, about, concerning
autour de, (a)round
de peur de, for fear of
en face de, opposite
hors de, out of
jusqu'à, up to, until
le long de, along
près de, near
quant à, as for

Using these prepositions wrongly is a source of frequent mistakes for the student. Here are some points to watch:

Verbs which Require no Preposition

attendre, to wait for	écouter, to listen to
chercher, to look for	espérer, to hope for
demander, to ask for	payer, to pay for

Do not put any prepositions after the above verbs. Attendre means "to wait *for*"; the "for" being included in the verb. Thus:

> Nous attendions le train. We were waiting *for* the train.
> Il va écouter la radio. He is going to listen *to* the wireless.
> Que cherchez-vous? What are you looking *for*?
> J'ai payé ma bicyclette. I've paid *for* my bicycle.

Uses of the Common Prepositions

Below you will find some notes on some of the prepositions already mentioned:

À may mean "to", "at" or "in": au jardin, to the garden, in the garden; à l'école, at school, to school; à mon retour, at, on my return. We find it before the names of towns: à Paris, to, at or in Paris; before masculine names of countries, au Pays de Galles, in or to Wales; au Portugal, au Japon, au Canada, aux États-Unis, in or to Portugal, Japan, Canada, the United States; as well as in aux Indes. It also has some idiomatic uses: à cheval, on horseback; à pied, on foot; à genoux, kneeling; à la main, in one's hand; au secours!, help!; au voleur!, stop thief!; au feu!, fire!; il a mal à la jambe, he has a pain in his leg; following this pattern we can make innumerable sentences like:

> Il a mal aux yeux. His eyes hurt.
> Il a mal au ventre. He has a pain in the stomach.
> Il a mal à la tête. His head aches.

It may express distance from a point:

Sidcup est à douze milles de Londres. Sidcup is (at) twelve miles from London.

It is found with verbs of taking away, stealing, borrowing, etc.:

Il a emprunté l'argent à son frère. He borrowed the money from his brother.
Il lui a pris le livre. He took the book from him.

À, too, describes a person's characteristics where in English we should write "with":

L'homme à la barbe noire. The man with the black beard.
La fille aux cheveux de lin. The girl with the flaxen hair.

For playing games we say "à":

Il joue au football, au rugby, au tennis. He plays (at) football, rugby, tennis.

Notice too expressions like **un verre à vin**, a wineglass (a glass *for* wine); **une cuiller à thé**, a teaspoon, and contrast with **un verre de vin**, a glass (full) of wine.

Avant, before (of time and order)

Il ne va pas rentrer avant sept heures. He won't be home before seven.
Je suis arrivé à l'arrêt avant lui. I arrived at the stop before him.

Avec, with (in the sense of "accompanied by")

Il est entré avec sa mère. He came in with his mother.

It is left out in sentences like:

He came in with his book in his hand. **Il entra son livre à la main.**

With a noun, it gives it an adverbial force: **avec soin,** with care, carefully; **avec patience,** patiently. It expresses "with" in connection with the use of an instrument:

Il l'a écrit avec son crayon. He wrote it with his pencil.
Elle m'a frappé avec un marteau. She hit me with a hammer.

Chez, at or to the house (shop, etc.) of

Chez moi, at, to my house, home.
Je vais chez le boulanger. I'm going to the baker's.
Elle est chez le curé. She's at the vicar's (house).

Also with authors' names.

Chez Racine, il y a beaucoup de passion. In Racine's work, there is much passion.

Dans, in, into, inside. Generally followed by an article or similar word: **dans le jardin, dans le livre, dans le sac. Dans la main** means "inside the hand", and could refer only to an object small enough to be enclosed in one's clasped hand; otherwise it is better to use **à la main:**

Il portait son chapeau à la main. He was carrying his hat in his hand.

Dans with an expression of time means "at the end of, after":

Dans deux jours je vais partir pour l'Amérique. In two days' time I'm leaving for America.

Dans is used before British counties, **dans le Kent,** in Kent. Notice too:

Il boit dans mon verre. He is drinking from my glass.
Il mange dans un bol. He is eating from a bowl.

A curious but logical idiom is:

Il prend l'argent dans sa poche. He takes the money from his pocket (the money was *in* his pocket when he took it!).

Dans is generally found after entrer:

Il entre dans la maison. He enters the house.

De, of, from, is the commonest French preposition, with a variety of meanings. Its most frequent occurrence is to translate the English apostrophe s; "John's book" is recast to "the book of John", le livre de Jean. Similarly, le chien de mon ami, my friend's dog. It also signifies origin—*from*; il vient de Nantes, he comes from Nantes. However, la route de Paris means "the road *to* Paris".

Most verbs of following, filling, covering, adorning, liking, etc., are followed by de: chargé de blé, laden with wheat; couvert de boue, covered with mud; aimé de tout le monde, loved by everyone; suivi de sa femme, followed by his wife. De generally translates "with" if followed by parts of the body:

Je l'ai vu de mes propres yeux. I saw it with my own eyes.

Many adjectives are followed by de; content d'être venu, pleased to have come; sûr de gagner, sure to win. When one verb is followed by the infinitive of another the most common preposition between them is de:

Je décidai de la suivre. I decided to follow her.
Nous avons offert de l'aider. We offered to help him.

De is used after superlatives; la plus belle maison de la région, the finest house in the region. One says too, de cette façon, in this fashion; d'une manière élégante, in an elegant manner; d'un ton froid, in a cold tone; de ce côté, in this direction; de l'autre côté, on the other side; sept heures du matin, du soir, seven o'clock in the morning, in the evening. De is also seen with musical instruments:

Il joue du piano, elle joue de la harpe. He plays the piano, she plays the harp.

It may also mean "about":

Il parle de ses aventures. He is speaking about his
adventures.

Depuis, since: depuis sa naissance, since his birth; depuis ce
jour-là, since that day. It is also used of place as well as
of time: depuis Paris jusqu'à Marseille, from Paris to
Marseilles. We have already mentioned its effect on
tenses (see pages 77 and 78):

Je suis ici depuis trois jours. I have been here for three
days (and I *am* still here).

Devant, before (of place): devant l'hôtel de ville, before the
town hall; devant le maire, in front of the mayor. It is
used with passer in sentences like this:

J'ai passé devant la maison ce matin. I passed the house
this morning.

En, in, must not be confused with dans. En expresses "to"
or "in" before the names of feminine countries: en Italie,
to or in Italy. En is used for "in" when it is followed
immediately by a noun: en France, in France; en été, in
summer; en danger, in danger; en colère, in anger; en
prison, in prison; en janvier, in January; en mil huit cent
soixante-quinze, in 1875; en voiture, by car. There are
only a few expressions where we see en with the article:
en l'absence de mon frère, in my brother's absence; en
l'an 1960, in the year 1960; sauter en l'air, to jump in the
air.

En draws attention to the material something is made
of:

Cette robe est en soie naturelle. This dress is made of
genuine silk.

En with an expression of time means "within":

Je le ferai en trois jours. I shall do it in three days (i.e., sometime within the next three days, it will be finished).

En may sometimes signify "as":

Il s'est déguisé en paysan. He disguised himself as a peasant.

Entre, between, among

Entre vous et moi. Between you and me.

Entre onze heures et midi. Between eleven and twelve o'clock.

J'ai remis la lettre entre les mains du directeur. I gave the letter into the hands of the manager (see **dans** above).

Environ, about (of numbers): **environ trente kilomètres,** about thirty kilometres.

Jusqu'à, up to, until, as far as

Je vais continuer mes efforts jusqu'au bout. I'm going to continue my efforts right up to the end.

Je voyage jusqu'à Londres. I'm travelling as far as London.

Jusqu'ici tout va bien. Up to now, all's well.

Not until is often rendered more suitably by **pas avant** (not before):

Il ne rentrera pas avant sept heures. He won't be home until seven.

Malgré, in spite of, despite

Malgré tout, je ferai mon devoir. Despite everything I shall do my duty.

Par, by, through

J'irai par la forêt. I shall go through the forest.

Par ici, monsieur! This way, sir!

Il regardait par la fenêtre. He was looking through the window.

Par négligence. Through negligence.

Je l'ai jeté par la fenêtre. I threw it out of the window.

Par is used with the instrument or agent of an action:

Il a été mordu par un chien. He was bitten by a dog.

Par is employed when speaking of the weather; **par un beau jour d'été,** on a fine summer's day; **par un temps superbe,** in superb weather, and to replace the English "a" in phrases such as **trois fois par jour,** three times a day; **deux fois par an,** twice a year. Remember that a tree falls **par terre,** to the ground, along the ground, since its roots are already there, while a stone falls **à terre** because it falls from a height.

Parmi, among(st): **Parmi ceux qui étaient là . . .** among those who were there . . .; **parmi les arbres,** among the trees.

Pendant, during: **pendant le voyage,** during the journey; **pendant mes vacances,** during my holidays.

Pour, for, in order to

Faites-le pour moi! Do it for me!

Ils partent pour Bruxelles. They are leaving for Brussels.

Je l'ai fait pour vous faire plaisir. I did it in order to please you.

With expressions of time, if the occasion is present or past, omit **pour:**

Il est resté trois jours chez moi. He stayed with me for three days.

Of future time **pour** returns:

Pour toujours! For ever!

Il sera à Paris pour trois jours. He will be in Paris for three days.

Sans, without

> **Sans votre aide.** Without your help.
> **Il est sans pitié.** He is pitiless.
> **Sans moi, il serait tombé.** Had it not been for me, he
> would have fallen.

Sauf, save, except for, apart from

> **Nous sommes tous ici, sauf Henri.** We are all here,
> except for Henri.

Selon, according to

> **L'Évangile selon Saint Luc.** The Gospel according to
> Saint Luke.
> **Selon lui, nous devons suivre ce sentier.** According to
> him, we must follow this path.
> **C'est selon.** It's all according.

Sous, under

> **Le chien est sous le lit.** The dog is under the bed.
> **Sous le règne de Louis XIV.** In the reign of Louis XIV.

Sur, on, on top of

> **La tasse est sur la table.** The cup is on the table.
> **Il prit une tasse sur la table.** He took a cup *from* the
> table (the cup was *on* the table when he took it).

Omit **sur** with expressions of time: **lundi,** on Monday;
le premier janvier, on the first of January. **Dix sur vingt,**
ten out of twenty.

> **La table a trois pieds de long sur deux de large.** The
> table is three feet long by two wide.

À travers, au travers de, through, across: **À travers le champ,**
across, through the field. Use **au travers de** when difficulties or obstacles are envisaged: **au travers des difficultés
de la guerre,** through the difficulties of war.

Vers, towards; about (with time of day)

> Je me dirigeai vers la maison. I moved towards the
> house.
> Nous y arriverons vers trois heures. We shall arrive
> there about three o'clock.

Repetition of Prepositions

The prepositions **de, à** and **en** are repeated before subsequent words:

> in Paris and London, **à Paris et à Londres**
> to France and Germany, **en France et en Allemagne**

Prepositions Used with Verbs

When two clauses have the same subject* a preposition
and an infinitive may be used:

> Après avoir consulté ma montre, je décidai de partir.
> After consulting my watch, I decided to leave.
> Je suis entré dans ma chambre sans faire de bruit. I
> went into my bedroom without making a noise.
> Avant de partir, je dis adieu à tout le monde. Before
> going I said goodbye to everyone.
> Pour réussir il faut bien travailler. You must work
> hard in order to succeed.
> Sans hésiter, il plongea dans la rivière. Without hesitat-
> ing he dived into the river.
> De peur d'être pris, ils se sauvèrent. For fear of being
> captured, they ran away.

Similar sentences may be made with the help of **à moins
de,** unless; **de crainte de,** for fear of; **afin de,** in order to.

You will have noticed that these prepositions are all
followed by an infinitive. In fact, only one preposition does

* If the two clauses have different subjects a conjunction must be
used. See the chapter on Conjunctions, page 143.

not govern the infinitive of the verb, that is EN, which is followed by the Present Participle.

> **En faisant ceci vous vous ferez détester.** By doing this, you will make yourself hated.

Note too that **après**, unlike the others, takes the Perfect Infinitive:

> **Après avoir consulté ma montre** . . . After consulting (having consulted) my watch . . .
>
> **Après avoir fini sa lettre** . . . After finishing (having finished) his letter . . .
>
> **Après s'être lavée, elle descendit.** After washing, she went downstairs.

CHAPTER VIII
CONJUNCTIONS

Conjunctions are words which join simple sentences together to make longer and more interesting ones. "When I arrived home, I discovered that I had left my key at the office" sounds much better than "I arrived home. I discovered something. I had left my key at the office". "When" is a conjunction or joining word.

Here is a list of conjunctions:

Co-ordinating Conjunctions

et, and
pourtant, however
ainsi, thus

ou, or
donc, therefore
aussi, and so

cependant, however
car, for
puis, then

Conjunctions of Time

quand
lorsque } when
après que, after
*avant que, before
aussitôt que
dès que } as soon as
depuis que, since
au moment où, just as

à peine . . . que, scarcely . . . than
tandis que
pendant que } while, whilst
tant que, as long as
*jusqu'à ce que, until
un jour que, one day when
le jour où, the day when

Conjunctions of Purpose

*afin que
*pour que } in order that
*de crainte que . . . ne
*de peur que . . . ne } lest

*sans que, without
*de sorte que, so that

Conditional

si, if   *à moins que . . . ne, unless
*pourvu que, provided that, if only

Concessive

*quoique ⎱
*bien que ⎰ although   *soit que . . . soit que, whether . . . or
                                quand même, even though

Causal

comme, as   attendu que ⎱
parce que, because   vu que   ⎰ seeing that
puisque, since

Comparative

à mesure que, in proportion as   selon que, according as
ainsi que, as, just as

Notes on the Above Conjunctions

1. The conjunctions marked with an asterisk are followed
by a verb in the Subjunctive Mood:

> Bien qu'il soit très pauvre, il est toujours heureux.
> Although he is very poor, he is always happy.

2. Some of the conjunctions have an expletive or untranslated ne which is put before the following verb:

> À moins qu'ils n'arrivent bientôt, nous sortirons sans
> eux. Unless they arrive soon, we shall go out without
> them.

3. You will have noticed that words like "after", "before",
"since", "because" may be prepositions or conjunctions.
When they are conjunctions a que is always added.

Prepositions.	Conjunctions.
après mon arrivée, after my arrival	**après que je fus arrivé,** after I had arrived
avant mon retour, before my return	**avant que je sois revenu,** before I returned
depuis sa naissance, since his birth	**depuis qu'il est né,** since he was born
à cause de lui, because of him	**parce qu'il était absent,** because he was absent

If the subject of both clauses is the same it is often preferable and easier to use a preposition with an infinitive or a noun. Thus say or write:

> **Avant de revenir j'ai fait des emplettes (purchases).**
> **Avant mon retour j'ai fait des emplettes.**

rather than

> **Avant que je sois revenu, j'ai fait des emplettes.**

Most of these conjunctions are quite simple to use. However, there are some points to note:

1. Be careful of the tenses after **quand, lorsque, après que, dès que, aussitôt que, tant que.**

(*a*) If any idea of future time is implied, the Future or Future Perfect must be employed in French:

> **Tant que je vivrai . . .** As long as I (shall) live . . .
> **Quand vous serez vieux, vous comprendrez mieux.** When you are (will be) old, you will understand better.
> **Après que vous aurez fini votre travail, vous pourrez vous amuser.** After you have (will have) finished your work, you will be able to enjoy yourself.
> **Dès que vous serez mort, on vous oubliera bien vite.** As soon as you are (will be) dead, you'll soon be forgotten.

(*b*) When **quand, lorsque, après que, dès que, aussitôt que** are used with a Past Tense, the Past Anterior follows the conjunction if the main verb in the other clause is in the Past Historic:

> Quand il *fut rentré*, il se coucha tout de suite. When he (had) got home, he went straight to bed.
>
> Après qu'il *eut* bien dîné, il résolut de lui écrire une lettre. After he had dined well, he determined to write him a letter.

A similar construction with à peine inverts the verb and pronoun:

> À peine l'eut-il fait qu'il se mit à regretter sa mauvaise action. Hardly had he done so than he began to regret his evil deed.

2. Puisque, depuis que, since. Puisque, since (because).

> Puisque vous êtes riche, il faut donner aux pauvres. Since you are rich, you must give to the poor.

Depuis que: since (from the time that). Be careful of the tense used after it. See the chapter on Verbs, pages 76–78.

> Depuis que vous êtes ici, tout va bien. Since you have been here, everything has been going well.

Here the Present Tense is employed since "you" *are* still here.

3. Quand même, even if, even though. Quand même is followed by a verb in the Conditional or Conditional Perfect:

> Quand même je l'aurais vu, je n'en aurais pas parlé. Even if I had seen it, I should not have spoken of it.

4. When a conjunction has two clauses under its influence, the conjunction need not be repeated if que is used in its place.

> Quand vous y arriverez et *que* vous verrez ma mère . . . When you get there and (when) you see my mother . . .

If the conjunction is **si** (if), the **que** is followed by the subjunctive:

> **S'il vient ici et qu'il vous voie . . .** If he comes here and (if he) sees you . . .

5. **Car,** for. Car means "for" in the sense of "because".

> **Vous pouvez tout faire car vous êtes le roi.** You can do anything, for you are the king.

Be careful not to use **pour** in cases like this.

6. **Aussi,*** so, and so, therefore. Aussi is followed by inversion of the verb and pronoun:

> **Aussi allez-vous revenir samedi.** So you are going to return on Saturday.

Another way of saying this is to put **donc** (therefore, then) either at the beginning of the sentence or after the verb:

> **Vous allez donc revenir samedi.**

7. **Tandis que, pendant que,** while, whilst. Pendant que is to be preferred to tandis que if the two actions described occur simultaneously:

> **Pendant qu'elle descendait la rue, la jeune fille lisait le journal.** While she was coming down the street, the girl was reading the paper.

Tandis que is best used when two statements are contrasted.

> **Vous, vous êtes riche, tandis que moi, je suis pauvre.** You are rich, whilst I am poor.

8. **Si** may mean both "if" and "whether". When it stands for "if" it is never followed by the Future or Conditional tenses:

> **S'il vient demain . . .** If he comes tomorrow . . . (Present).

* Aussi may also be an adverb meaning "also", "too".

S'il venait demain ... If he $\left.\begin{array}{l}\text{came} \\ \text{were to come}\end{array}\right\}$ tomorrow
... (Imperfect).

However, the Future and Conditional are allowed when **si** means "whether".

Je ne sais pas s'il viendra. I do not know whether (if) he will come.

Tenses after SI, If

At this stage, it is worth while considering the possible combinations of tenses when **si**, if, is used:

Present and Future:

S'il vient ce soir, je serai content. If he comes tonight, I shall be pleased.

Imperfect and Conditional:

S'il venait ce soir, je serais content. If he $\left.\right\}$ $\begin{array}{l}\text{were to come} \\ \text{came}\end{array}$ tonight, I should be pleased.

Pluperfect and Conditional Perfect:

S'il était venu ce soir, j'aurais été content. If he had come tonight, I should have been pleased.

CHAPTER IX

THE WEATHER, TIME OF DAY, AGES, DATES, SEASONS, L'AN, ANNO DOMINI, MEASUREMENT, FRACTIONS, COLLECTIVE AND APPROXIMATE NUMBERS, PRICE, DISTANCE, FEELINGS

The Weather

In every discussion about the weather we generally find the verb faire and not the verb être. The usual pattern is to use impersonally the 3rd Person of the verb faire together with a descriptive adjective.

Il fait beau. It is fine, the weather is fine.
Il fait mauvais. The weather is bad.
Il fait froid. It is cold.
Il fait frais. It is cool.

All these answer the question:

Quel temps fait-il? What is the weather like?

It is, of course, possible to make use of this pattern in any tense:

Il fera froid demain. It will be cold tomorrow.
Il faisait froid hier. It was cold yesterday.
Il a fait froid en Suisse. The weather was cold in Switzerland.

Other idiomatic expressions of similar pattern are:

Il fait un temps merveilleux. The weather is marvellous.
Il fait doux. The weather is mild.
Il fait lourd. The weather is close.
Il fait sombre. It's dark, dull.
Il fait du vent. It's windy.
Il fait du soleil. It's sunny.
Il fait du brouillard. It's foggy.

Il fait jour. It's daylight.
Il fait nuit. It's dark (night-time).
Il fait clair de lune. There's moonlight.
Il pleut. It's raining.

One can also make sentences of the type:

Le temps est beau. The weather is fine.
Le temps est mauvais. The weather is bad.

The Time of Day: L'HEURE

The word for "time of day" is heure and not temps,* and so "What time is it?" must be translated as Quelle heure est-il?

The answer to this question is given in "heures" (hours):

Il est une heure. It's one o'clock (lit. one hour).
Il est deux heures. It's two o'clock.
Il est trois heures. It's three o'clock.

and so on until we get to:

Il est midi. It's twelve o'clock (noon).
Il est minuit. It's twelve o'clock (midnight).

Please do not say, "Il est douze heures"!

"Half past" is expressed by adding et demie (when heure is mentioned) and et demi (after midi and minuit, which are masculine):

Il est une heure et demie. It's half past one.
Il est deux heures et demie. It's half past two.
Il est trois heures et demie. It's half past three.

but

Il est midi et demi. It's half past twelve (noon).
Il est minuit et demi. It's half past twelve (midnight).

The word demi (half) is an adjective, and so will agree with heure (f.) or midi or minuit (m.).

* Avez-vous l'heure? Have you the time? With the answer "It's two o'clock, etc.". Avez-vous le temps? Have you time (to spare to do something for someone)?

A "quarter past" and a "quarter to" are expressed by adding **et quart** or **moins le (un) quart** respectively.

Il est quatre heures et quart. It's a quarter past four.

Il est quatre heures moins le quart. ⎫ It's a quarter to
                      moins un quart. ⎭ four.

Minutes past the hour are indicated by adding **une, deux, trois, quatre,** etc. The French word "minute" is feminine, and that is why we say **une.**

Il est onze heures une. It's a minute past eleven.
Il est onze heures cinq. It's five past eleven.
Il est trois heures vingt. It's twenty past three.

The usage is similar to our railway time-tables: 11.1, 11.5, 3.20, etc.

Minutes to the hour are shown by **moins une, moins deux,** etc. **Moins** really means "less", so we are doing a little subtraction; "five to eleven" becomes "eleven hours minus five (minutes)".

Il est quatre heures moins dix. It's ten to four.
Il est neuf heures moins vingt-cinq. It's twenty-five to nine.

Some idiomatic expressions of time worth learning are:

À trois heures précises, at three o'clock exactly
vers une heure, about one o'clock
Il est dix heures environ. It's about ten o'clock.
Il est près de cinq heures. It's nearly five o'clock.
dix heures du matin, 10 a.m.
six heures du soir, 6 p.m.
une heure, an hour
une demi-heure, half an hour
un quart d'heure, a quarter of an hour
trois quarts d'heure, three-quarters of an hour.

On railway time-tables a twenty-four-hour system is found:

Départ à 22 h. Departure at 10 p.m.

Ages

The important thing to remember is that in French one *has* an age: one uses the verb avoir and not être.

> Quel âge avez-vous? How old are you?
> J'ai vingt ans. I am twenty.

Notice that in the reply the word ans, years, must be given. If you say J'ai vingt a Frenchman would ask himself what you have twenty of!

Try to learn these useful expressions too:

> un homme d'un certain âge, a middle-aged man
> une femme de trente ans, a thirty-year-old woman
> Je suis plus âgé que lui de six ans. I am six years older than he (older by six years).
> Elle a passé la cinquantaine. She's past fifty.

Dates and Expressions of Time

Dates

> Quelle date sommes-nous?
> Quel jour est-ce?
> Quel jour sommes-nous? } What is the date?
> Le combien sommes-nous?

For the first day of the month we use le premier; for all the others we use the cardinal numbers, deux, trois, quatre, etc.

> C'est (nous sommes) le premier mai. It's the first of May.
> le deux mars, the second of March
> le dix octobre, the tenth of October
> le vingt décembre, the twentieth of December

The names of the months are janvier, février, mars, avril, mai, juin, juillet, août, septembre, octobre, novembre, décembre, all spelt with a small letter, as are also the days of the week, dimanche (Sunday), lundi, mardi, mercredi, jeudi, vendredi, samedi. If we want to give an exact date we can say something like this: le lundi onze janvier, Monday January 11 (notice the word order).

Useful Expressions of Time

en janvier, au mois de janvier, in January

Quel jour de la semaine est-ce? What day of the week is it?

C'est jeudi. It's Thursday.

samedi, on Saturday

le samedi, on Saturdays

mercredi soir, on Wednesday evening

tous les vendredis, every Friday

lundi prochain, next Monday

mardi dernier, last Tuesday

il y a huit jours, a week ago

il y a quinze jours, a fortnight ago

la semaine dernière, last week

la semaine prochaine, next week (of future time)

la semaine suivante, the following (next) week (of past time)

La semaine prochaine je vais en Bretagne. Next week I'm going to Brittany.

La semaine suivante il reçut une lettre de son père. The next (following) week he received a letter from his father.

hier soir, last night (yesterday evening)

cette nuit, last night (the time you slept!)

Hier soir j'ai regardé la télévision. Last night I watched television.

Cette nuit je n'ai pas bien dormi. Last night I did not sleep well.

ce soir, this evening, tonight

ce soir-là, that evening

le matin, in the morning

le soir, in the evening

Le matin je travaille, le soir je lis un livre. In the morning I work, in the evening I read a book.

Notice no preposition is needed with expressions of time: **le matin**, *in* the morning; **jeudi**, *on* Thursday; **le deux septembre**, *on* the second of September.

The Seasons: LES SAISONS (f.)

The names of the seasons, starting with Spring, are **le printemps**, **l'été**, **l'automne**, **l'hiver**: they are masculine. We say **au printemps**, in Spring but **en été, en automne, en hiver**; in Summer, in Autumn, in Winter.

Year: L'AN (m.), L'ANNÉE (f.)

"Year" is, in French, either **l'an** (m.) or **l'année** (f.). The distinction between them is often a matter of which sounds better in a sentence. This will not help a learner very much, so here are two points of difference. With a cardinal number use **an: quatre ans**, four years; with an ordinal it is better to put **année; la quatrième année**, the fourth year. Moreover, **l'année** not only marks a point in time but also emphasises the *content* of the year.

Toute cette année j'ai travaillé dur. I've worked hard all this year.

Similarly, **jour, matin, soir** have feminine forms **journée, matinée, soirée**.

Anno Domini

There is not much difficulty about this in French. If we wish to give the year we form it more or less as we do in English: in 1960, **en dix-neuf cent soixante**. However, we can also say **en mil neuf cent soixante** (in one thousand nine hundred and sixty). This is not the usual spelling of **mille**, but after the year 1000, **l'an mille**, the spelling **mil** and not **mille** is used for dates.

Dimensions

There are three ways of translating into French the sentence "This table is two metres long".:

(1) **Cette table est longue de deux mètres.** This table is long by two metres.

(2) **Cette table a deux mètres de long (de longueur).** This table has two metres of length.

(3) **Cette table a une longueur de deux mètres.** This table has a length of two metres (rarely used).

Similar constructions may be used for width and length. Thus "This table is two metres wide":

Cette table a deux mètres de large (de largeur).
Cette table est large de deux mètres.
Cette table a une largeur de deux mètres.

Now to combine length and width we use the preposition **sur:**

Cette table a deux mètres de long *sur* deux de large. This table is two metres long by two metres wide.

De is used before a numeral to express the measure of difference in comparisons of sizes, ages, etc.

Mon frère est plus grand que moi de dix centimètres. My brother is ten centimetres taller than I (taller by 10 centimetres).

Fractions

The most common fractions you are likely to need are **un demi**, a half; **un tiers**, a third; **un quart**, a quarter. With these we can make other fractions like **deux tiers**, two-thirds; **trois quarts**, three-quarters. For the remaining numbers we use the ordinals: **un cinquième**, a fifth; **un sixième**, a sixth; **un septième**, a seventh, etc. We can then form fractions like **quatre septièmes**, four-sevenths.

Notice these common expressions:

il est à moitié (à demi) mort, he is half dead
trois sur quatre, three out of four
dix sur vingt, ten out of twenty
neuf fois sur dix, nine times out of ten

Collective and Approximate Numbers

une paire de gants, a pair of gloves

To make a definite number like vingt, twenty, into an approximate one, add -aine, une vingtaine, about twenty.

cent livres, a hundred books
une centaine de livres, about a hundred books
des centaines de livres, hundreds of books
une vingtaine d'hommes, about a score of men
une femme d'une trentaine d'années, a woman of about
    thirty

All these collectives are feminine nouns and are followed by de, like other expressions of quantity:

une douzaine d'œufs, a dozen eggs

The indefinite number for mille (thousand) is un millier (about a thousand).

Des milliers de mouches. Thousands of flies. (You are not likely to know the exact number!)

Price

We have already mentioned in the chapter on the articles that the French use the Definite Article after a price:

trois francs la bouteille, le mètre, la douzaine, la pièce, three francs a bottle, a metre, a dozen, a piece (each)

There are also a few idiomatic expressions of buying and selling which are worth learning:

Le prix de ce chapeau est de quarante francs. The price of this hat is forty francs.

Nous l'avons payé dix francs. We paid ten francs for it.

Elle l'a vendu vingt francs. She sold it for twenty francs.

On m'en a demandé cent francs. They charged me 100 francs for it.

Distance and Speed

One should, of course, be able to ask how far it is to a town and to answer a similar question. Here is a pattern:

Quelle distance y a-t-il d'ici à Verneuil? How far is it from here to Verneuil.

D'ici à Verneuil il y a vingt kilomètres. It's twenty kilometres from here to Verneuil.

cent kilomètres à l'heure, a hundred kilometres an hour.

L'auto faisait du cent à l'heure. The car was doing a hundred (kilometres!).

Feelings

To describe personal feelings of heat, cold, etc., the verb avoir is used in the following expressions:

avoir chaud: il a chaud. He is (feels) warm.

avoir froid: Nous avons froid. We are (feel) cold.

avoir sommeil: J'ai sommeil. I am (feel) sleepy.

avoir faim: J'avais faim. I was (felt) hungry.

avoir soif: Avez-vous soif? Are you thirsty?

avoir peur: Il a peur de moi. He's afraid of me.

avoir envie: J'ai envie d'y aller. I feel like going there.

With these expressions avoir froid, avoir chaud, when there is no question of a feeling of cold or warmth but of actual temperature, the verb être is substituted for avoir.

En hiver l'eau de la piscine est froide. In winter the water in the swimming-pool is cold.

Cette soupe est très chaude. This soup is very hot.

CHAPTER X

INTERJECTIONS

Interjections are words or sounds used to express feelings of joy, sorrow, amazement, annoyance, to give orders, attract attention or to imitate various noises. We give here but a few of them: the student will be able to collect many more if he keeps his ears open on his travels.

To show joy or displeasure you vary the tone of **Ah!** **Eh!** **Hi!** or **Oh!** while **Aïe** signifies disapproval (generally repeated three times!). To call someone or to elicit attention one says **Hé!** **Pst!** or **Holà!** Disgust is expressed by **Fi!** or **Pouah!** **Allons!** means "Come on now!" and gives encouragement as does also the word **Courage!** You cannot go far without coming across **Attention!**, Mind your step!, or **Halte!**, Stop!, or **Gare!**, Watch out! To enjoin silence one may try **Paix!** or **Silence!** If you wish to show special approval you can call **Bravo!** or **Très bien!**, while to encore a singer you can shout **Bis!** **Mon Dieu!**, **Parbleu!**, **Ma foi!**, **Dame** and **Pardi** (in the South) are mild swear words used to enforce something you want to say. When you are chopping wood you can make the noise **Han!** to show that you are working very hard.

To imitate sounds is not as easy as you might think. French guns go **Pan!** **Pan!** and not "Bang! Bang!"; a French fist as it strikes gives the sound **Toc!**, a slap on the face **Vlan!** After this, you will not be surprised to hear that Gallic ducks say **Coin!** **Coin!** (not "Quack! Quack!"), a French locomotive makes a noise like **Teuf!** and a cockerel sings **Coquerico!** Any student would find great interest in collecting a list of these interjections. Here are two to start with: **Oh là là!** (untranslatable!) and **Hein?** (used to make a statement into a question):

Vous aimez ça, hein? You like that, eh?

CHAPTER XI

WORD ORDER IN FRENCH

The Usual Order

As a general rule, the question of the order in which to arrange the words in a French sentence presents little difficulty. French and English are very similar in usage, and the exceptions to normal procedure have already been mentioned in previous chapters. However, we shall now try to bring together the more important deviations as a handy reference for the reader.

Inversion of Subject and Verb

The usual position of the subject is before the verb, but in the following cases there is inversion:

(a) *Questions, Exclamations, Wishes.* Here the subject follows the verb:

> Où allez-vous? Where are you going?
> Jean, est-il arrivé? Has John arrived?
> Vive le roi! Long live the King!
> Puissiez-vous être heureux! May you be happy!

(b) Dit-il, *etc.* After reported conversation there is inversion of such verbs as dire, répondre, crier, s'écrier, songer, penser, sembler.

> «Comment vous portez-vous?» demanda-t-elle. "How are you?" she asked.
> «Très bien, merci» répondit-il. "Very well, thank you," he replied.

Que, ce que, comme, lorsque, quand. You may sometimes find inversion of subject and verb after the relative pronouns que and ce que, and the conjunctions que, comme, lorsque and quand:

Le séjour qu'ont bâti mes aïeux . . . The dwelling which
my ancestors built . . .

Comme dormait Jacob . . . As Jacob slept . . .

Quand on est jeune et que fleurit le printemps . . . When
one is young and when spring is in bloom . . .

The inversion here is a matter of style only. It is quite
correct not to make it.

À peine, aussi, peut-être. There is inversion of normal
order after the conjunctions à peine, scarcely, hardly; aussi,
and so, therefore; also after peut-être, perhaps, and sometimes after en vain, in vain.

Il était fatigué; aussi se coucha-t-il immédiatement.
He was tired, so he went to bed straightaway.

Peut-être viendra-t-il vous voir demain. Perhaps he will
come and see you tomorrow.

Object of an Infinitive Dependent on FAIRE

When an infinitive is used after the verbs faire, entendre,
voir, laisser, if the object of these verbs is a noun, you should
place it after the infinitive and not between the verbs as in
English:

Il fait travailler *ses hommes*. He makes *his men* work.
Je vois venir *le docteur*. I see *the doctor* coming.

When the object is a pronoun we have the normal order:

Il les fait travailler. He makes them work.
Je le vois venir. I see him coming.

Preposition at the End of a Sentence or Clause

In French you may not finish with a preposition. A
sentence like "Whom were you talking to?" must be changed
to "To whom were you talking?" before it can be translated:

À qui parliez-vous? Whom were you talking to?
Avec quoi l'avez-vous fait? What did you make it with?

DONT

After **DONT** the subject, verb and complement must follow in that order. Thus a phrase like "the man whose son I saw yesterday" must be changed to "the man of whom I saw the son yesterday", l'homme dont j'ai vu le fils hier.

Now study carefully these sentences:

> **Mon frère dont vous lisez le livre** . . . My brother whose book you are reading (of whom you are reading the book) . . .
>
> **Un auteur dont j'aime les romans** . . . An author whose novels I like (of whom I like the novels).

JAMAIS

Even if **jamais** begins a sentence, the word order still remains subject, verb and the rest of the sentence:

> **Jamais enfant ne fut plus gâté que lui.** Never was a child more spoiled than he.

COMME and QUE

In a sentence beginning with "how" used in an exclamatory sense there is no such inversion as there is in English:

> **Comme elle est belle!** How beautiful she is!
>
> **Qu'il fait mauvais!** How wretched the weather is!

Position of Adverb

The adverb either follows the verb or, if there is need for emphasis, comes first in the sentence. It does not come between the subject and the verb. Always say "he walks slowly" or "slowly he walks" and never "he slowly walks".

> **Il vient bien souvent chez nous.** } He comes to us very
> **Bien souvent il vient chez nous.** } often.

In a compound tense short adverbs usually precede the Past Participle, others follow:

J'ai trop vu. I have seen too much.

Elle y est allée régulièrement. She went there regularly.

Word Order in Questions

(a) When the subject of the verb is a personal pronoun, the pronoun follows the verb:

Va-t-*il* chanter ce soir? Is he going to sing tonight?

Aimez-*vous* le café? Do you like coffee?

Êtes-*vous* allé en France? Did you go to France?

N'acceptent-*ils* pas? Are they not accepting?

(b) When the subject is a noun the subject is put first, then the verb followed by the corresponding personal pronoun:

Votre frère va-t-il nous aider? Is your brother going to help us?

Quand la lettre est-elle arrivée? When did the letter arrive?

Vous et votre ami êtes-vous allés en Suisse? Did you and your friend go to Switzerland?

Of course, in colloquial French the above inversion may be avoided by using est-ce que? In this way the normal order of subject, verb and the rest of the sentence is preserved. Here are the above examples rewritten, using est-ce que . . .:

Est-ce que votre frère va nous aider?

Quand est-ce que la lettre est arrivée?

Est-ce que vous et votre ami êtes allés en Suisse?

Questions containing pronouns may be turned the same way:

Est-ce qu'il va chanter ce soir?

Est-ce que vous aimez le café?

Est-ce qu'ils n'acceptent pas?

CHAPTER XII

CONSTRUCTIONS WITH FRENCH VERBS

Although French and English usage are often very similar, we cannot always assume that this is so. Let us give an example. In English the same verb may frequently be used transitively or intransitively.

> The water *boils*. Intransitive (i.e., having no object).
> I *boil* the water. Transitive (i.e., "water" is the object of "boil").

When we translate these two sentences into French, we notice at once a great difference:

> L'eau bout. The water boils.
> Je fais bouillir l'eau. I boil the water. (I make the water boil.)

Only a very compendious dictionary containing a host of examples will give complete satisfaction to the student. Failing this and even better from the learner's point of view, a careful note should be made of the construction employed with a verb every time any reading of French books takes place.

It is impossible to cover the whole range of French verbs in a chapter. We shall have to be content with an outline of the main points.

Completion of the Meaning of a Verb

In English we may use the word "open" in two ways:

> I *open* the door (transitively).
> The door *opens* (intransitively).

To the French the second sentence seems incomplete. A verb like "open" is generally used with an object; one opens something. The Frenchman expects an object: in the sentence "The door opens", he asks "The door opens what?"

To this question the only possible answer is "The door opens *itself*" and the verb becomes reflexive:

> **J'ouvre la porte.** I open the door.
> **La porte s'ouvre.** The door opens.

Here are some further examples of the same process:

> **Je vends l'article.** I sell the article.
> **L'article se vend bien.** The article sells (itself) well.
> **Il arrête l'auto.** He stops the car.
> **L'auto s'arrête.** The car stops (itself).
> **La mère lave le plancher.** The mother washes the floor.
> **La mère se lave.** The mother washes (herself).
> **Le barbier rasait un client.** The barber was shaving a customer.
> **Le barbier se rasait.** The barber was shaving (himself).

Verbs with Two Objects

Verbs like "teach", "show", "tell" have two objects:

> "I teach him French."
> "He showed me a card."
> "I tell the children stories."

One of these objects must be indirect, and the word "to" has to be added. The sentences will now read:

> "I teach French to him."
> "He showed a card to me."
> "I tell stories to the children."

Always remember to insert "to" before translating into French:

> I teach him French. (I teach French to him.) **Je lui apprends le français.**
> I wish the boy a good journey. (I wish a good journey to the boy.) **Je souhaite un bon voyage au garçon.**
> We told them a good story. (We told a good story to them.) **Nous leur avons raconté une bonne histoire.**

They refuse him permission. (They refuse permission to him.) Ils lui refusent la permission.

I gave the girl a present. (I gave a present to the girl.) J'ai donné un cadeau à la fillette.

The following verbs are used similarly:

confier quelque chose à quelqu'un, to entrust something to someone

demander quelque chose à quelqu'un, to ask someone for something

Nous avons demandé un verre de lait au fermier. We asked the farmer for a glass of milk.

dire quelque chose à quelqu'un $\left\{\begin{array}{l}\text{to say something to someone} \\ \text{to tell someone something}\end{array}\right.$

Je lui ai dit adieu. I said farewell to him.
Elle m'a dit le mot. She told me the word.

pardonner quelque chose à quelqu'un, to forgive someone something

Pardonnez-nous nos offenses. Forgive us our trespasses.

rendre quelque chose à quelqu'un, to give something back to someone

Nous lui rendrons le cadeau. We shall give him back the present.

Verbs Which Require no Prepositions

Some verbs do not need to be followed by a preposition:

attendre, to wait for: J'attends l'autobus.
chercher, to look for: Il cherchait la maison.
demander, to ask for: Nous demandons du sucre.
écouter, to listen to: Vous écoutez la radio.
espérer, to hope for: J'espérais la paix.
payer, to pay for: Mon père a payé la bicyclette.
regarder, to look at: Regardez cet arbre!

Verbs Which Are Followed by À Before a Noun

jouer à, to play (a game): J'ai joué au tennis.

obéir à, to obey: Obéissez à vos parents.

penser à, to think of (turn one's thoughts to): À quoi pensez-vous?

répondre à, to answer: Répondez à cette question!

ressembler à, to resemble: Il ressemblait à son oncle.

Some Verbs Are Followed by DE

s'approcher de, to approach: Ils s'approchèrent de la maison.

changer de, to change: Il a changé de caractère.

jouer de, to play (a musical instrument): Vous aimez jouer du piano.

manquer de, to lack: Elle manque de tact.

penser de, to think (have an opinion): Que pensez-vous de ce tableau?

ENTRER DANS Before a Noun

Ils entrèrent dans la maison. They entered the house.

Verbs of "Taking Away"

These put à before the person interested:

acheter quelque chose à quelqu'un, to buy something from someone

cacher quelque chose à quelqu'un, to hide something from someone

emprunter quelque chose à quelqu'un, to borrow something from someone

ôter quelque chose à quelqu'un, to take away something from someone

prendre quelque chose à quelqu'un, to take something from someone

voler quelque chose à quelqu'un, to steal something from someone

Il m'a pris le livre. He took the book from me.

Ils ont volé de l'argent à leur ami. They stole money from their friend.

Il emprunta dix livres à son père. He borrowed £10 from his father.

During your reading you should keep a careful watch. Note carefully how each verb is used and if possible write the sentence down and learn it.

Government of Verbs

As we have already mentioned, when two verbs are used together in French the second is put into the Infinitive and the two verbs are linked by the prepositions à, de, par. There may even be no preposition at all between them. Here are a few examples:

Il aime à chanter. He loves singing.

Nous essayons de comprendre. We are trying to understand.

Il finira par accepter. He will end up by accepting.

Je voudrais bien entrer. I should like to come in.

On page 87 you will find a list of verbs together with the preposition required. Of course, it is not possible to include every possible verb. The student should keep his eyes open when reading French to note down each new construction.

"Come and See", "Go and Fetch"

Do not use et between a verb and the following infinitive when you are writing down verbs of motion.

Go and fetch the doctor. Allez chercher le docteur.

He came and saw me often. Il venait souvent me voir.

Demander à quelqu'un de faire quelque chose

A very common group is the one which follows the above pattern. Here is a useful list of these verbs:

commander à quelqu'un de faire quelque chose, to command someone to do something

conseiller à quelqu'un de faire quelque chose, to advise someone to do something

défendre à quelqu'un de faire quelque chose, to forbid someone to do something

demander à quelqu'un de faire quelque chose, to ask someone to do something

dire à quelqu'un de faire quelque chose, to tell someone to do something

ordonner à quelqu'un de faire quelque chose, to order someone to do something

permettre à quelqu'un de faire quelque chose, to permit someone to do something

persuader à quelqu'un de faire quelque chose, to persuade someone to do something

promettre à quelqu'un de faire quelque chose, to promise someone to do something

Il avait permis à ses enfants d'y aller. He had permitted his children to go there.

Vous avez déjà dit à ce monsieur de ne pas entrer. You have already told this gentleman not to come in.

Promettez-moi de ne pas le faire. Promise me not to do it.

"To go in, out, up, down, away, across, on"

to go in, entrer

Il entra dans la maison. He went into the house.

to go out, sortir

Elle sortait du cinéma. She was going out of the cinema.

to go up, monter
   Montez dans votre chambre. Go up to your room.
to go down, descendre
   Il descendit dans le trou. He went down into the hole.
to go away, partir
   Elle partit sans me dire adieu. She went away without
      saying goodbye to me.
to go across, traverser
   Nous traversons le pont. We cross the bridge.
to go on, continuer
   Il continua de parler. He went on speaking.